In Order of Appearance . . .

Ninette de Valois
Frederick Ashton
Andy Warhol
Vincent van Gogh
Theaster Gates
Bridget Riley
Roy Lichtenstein
David Ogilvy
Marina Abramović
Gilbert & George
Caravaggio
Picasso
J. J. Abrams
Piero della Francesca
Luc Tuymans
Johannes Vermeer
Peter Doig
Rembrandt
Kerry James Marshall
Michelangelo
Ai Weiwei
David Hockney
Marcel Duchamp
Bob and Roberta Smith

Think

Like an

Artist

and Lead a More
Creative, Productive Life

Will Gompertz

Abrams Image, New York

By the same author
What Are You Looking At?

Editor: Michael Sand
Designer: Darilyn Lowe Carnes
Production Manager: Anet Sirna-Bruder

Library of Congress Control Number: 2015957311

ISBN: 978-1-4197-2183-0

First published in the United Kingdom by Penguin Books Ltd.

Printed and bound in the United States
10 9 8 7 6 5 4 3 2 1

Abrams Image books are available at special discounts when purchased in quantity
for premiums and promotions as well as fundraising or educational use.
Special editions can also be created to specification. For details, contact
specialsales@abramsbooks.com or the address below.

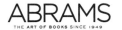

115 West 18th Street
New York, NY 10011
www.abramsbooks.com

In memoriam

Steve Hare

PREFACE

We cannot all paint like Picasso or sculpt like Michelangelo, but we can all think like an artist.

When Marcel Duchamp asked, "Why does art have to be beautiful?" in 1917, he changed art forever. You or I could have done that. And we could have sparked an entire art movement like Damien Hirst did in 1991 by convincing an art dealer to pay to put a dead shark in a tank of formaldehyde.

Even the mighty Cézanne is within our reach. He realized in the late nineteenth century that a subject shown from two different viewpoints in the same painting appeared more urgent and honest. Why? Because that's how we see: with two eyes, not one. It was the insight that led to modernism in all its forms. We could have figured that out.

So, why don't we come up with great ideas if they're so easy? Well, we can. And my hope is that this book will help show you how.

INTRODUCTION

Creativity is a hot topic. It is a subject that's exciting politicians, academics and wise men and women the world over. They say it is very important. That it will be central to our future prosperity. Which is all well and good. But what exactly is creativity and how does it work?

And why do some people appear to find it easy to come up with brilliant, fresh ideas while others don't? Is it simply a case of "creative types" being programmed differently, or does it have more to do with behavior and attitude?

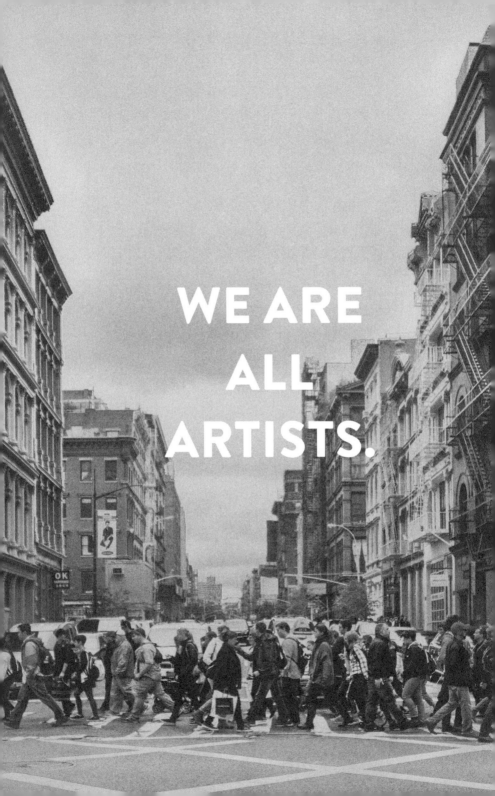

We are a uniquely imaginative species. Our ability to conceive complex ideas and realize them requires a series of cognitive processes that are beyond the capability of any other life form or any machine. For us, it's no big deal. We do it all the time, from preparing a meal to texting a witty message to a friend. We might consider them mundane tasks but they still require us to imagine, to be creative. It's a fantastic natural gift which, when cultivated properly, can enable us to achieve the most extraordinary things.

Using our imagination enlivens and enriches our minds and our life experience. We come into our own when we exercise our brains, when we think. I have never met an artist of any type who is indifferent or incurious. The same goes for successful chefs, gardeners and sports coaches; anybody in fact who has a zest for their subject and a willingness to innovate. They have a brightness in their eyes that radiates a palpable life force. Being creative has that effect.

The act of making and creating is deeply satisfying, life-affirming and rewarding.

So how do we go about harnessing this innate talent? How can we take our creativity off autopilot to generate those bold original concepts that could add value to our lives and maybe even to the wider world? And, more specifically, how do we trigger our imagination to conjure up the innovative thoughts that could be turned into something material and worthwhile?

I've been thinking about these questions for the best part of three decades. At first it was because new ideas and talented people fascinated me. And then it became part of my job as a publisher, producer, writer, broadcaster and journalist working in the arts.

I've had the privilege of being able to observe and meet some of the greatest exponents of creative thinking today, from the audacious British artist Damien Hirst to the multi-Oscar-winning American actress Meryl Streep. Obviously, they are all different, but in one regard, at least, not quite as different as you might imagine.

Over the years it has become pretty evident to me that there are a handful of clearly identifiable traits that are common to all successful creative people, from novelists and film directors to scientists and philosophers. I'm not talking about fanciful otherworldly qualities, but the basic practices and processes that allow their talents to flourish. Practices and processes which, if adopted, could help the rest of us unleash our own latent creativity.

And creative talent is something we all have, of that there is no doubt. True, some people may be more adept at composing music than others, but that doesn't immediately render the non-composers "uncreative." The fact is we are all perfectly capable of being artists of one type or another. Each and every one of us has the capacity to conceptualize, to step out of time and space and consider instead a range of abstract ideas and associations that are unrelated to each other or the present moment. We do it when we are daydreaming, or speculating, or even when we are telling lies.

> **Confidence is crucial. Artists don't seek permission to paint or write or act or sing; they just do it.**

The problem is, some of us have either convinced ourselves that we are not creative, or are yet to find our way. Confidence in our own creativity can wane. Which is bad. Confidence is crucial. In my experience artists, like a lot of us, fear being "found out." But somehow they manage to summon up enough self-belief to overcome the self-doubt, which enables them to back their creativity. The Beatles were just a bunch of young lads with time on their hands who found the confidence to persuade themselves and then the world that they were musicians.

They didn't wait to be asked. Artists don't seek permission to paint or write or act or sing; they just do it. What tends to set them apart, and gives them their power and purpose, is not their creativity per se—we all have that. Rather, it's the fact that they have found a focus for it, an area of interest that has fired their imagination and provided a vehicle for their talents.

It's a phenomenon I first witnessed back in the 1980s when I was in my early twenties and working as a stagehand at Sadler's Wells Theatre in London. This was at a time before I had discovered art or, indeed, much else. But I did find myself drawn to the theater's mix of practical crafts and acts of illusion.

It was always hard work before and during the show, but once the final curtain had come down and the audience had departed we would leave en masse for a relaxing drink in the pub. In due course the show's cast and "creatives" would join us there. This was the time when the strict hierarchies that exist in the theater were removed. Rank and regiment were now irrelevant, and I would occasionally find myself sitting next to a revered legend, typically from the world of ballet (the theater's forte).

One night it might be the grand Dame Ninette de Valois—once of Diaghilev's legendary Ballets Russes and subsequently the founder of the Royal Ballet. On another, it could be Sir Frederick Ashton, the master choreographer, who would share the latest gossip while tapping the rim of his chilled glass of Chablis. For a naive young lad, brought up in rural England, such nights were wonderfully intoxicating and exotic.

This was when I first encountered what you might call bona-fide "artists," those independent spirits who earn a good living and a big reputation by making things up. Even in the down-to-earth surroundings of a rough London pub they stood out. De Valois and Ashton attracted attention without seeking it, and rarely had to face the indignity of being interrupted. They had this inner strength that was so resolute and forceful it transmitted an outer confidence that overwhelmed and beguiled.

It is by being creative that we are likely to find contentment in our digitized age.

They weren't superhuman. They were as full of foibles and insecurities as the rest of us. But they had found the thing—dance in their case—that turned their imagination on and enabled them to exploit the superhuman gift of creativity we all share. But how did they find it? How did they nurture it? And what can they teach us?

This book is my attempt to answer those questions, informed by observations made while inhabiting a world of writers, musicians, directors and actors. The aim is to shed a little light on how the creative elite fires its imagination and uses it as a productive tool.

There is much to learn from them all, but perhaps it is fine artists—by which I mean painters and sculptors, video-makers and performance practitioners—who can teach us most about the creative process. There is a singularity to the way they work that makes it easier to pin down how a creative mind thinks when operating at maximum capacity.

Hence the title of the book. Each of the main chapters takes one particular approach, or attitude, that strikes me as being essential to the creative process, and explores it through an artist's experience. Not the technical specifics, like how to prime a canvas or paint light, but the ways of working and thinking that enable them to excel creatively. Ways that can be universally applied to anyone wanting to get creative.

Personally, I think that will be more and more of us in the future, as we react to the disrupting effects of the digital revolution. In many respects recent technological advances have been exciting and liberating: The Internet has made it much easier to source materials and information, to meet like-minded individuals and create networks. And it has provided a cheap and easy global platform for us to market our wares. All of which can help support our creative endeavors.

But there's a downside too: it's a little overwhelming. For all the benefits the Internet age has brought, buying us more time hasn't been one of them. Life has become ridiculously busy. Our day-to-day existence is more frenetic than ever. Not only are there still the same old chores to do, but now when we sit down to relax there is an avalanche of text messages, e-mails, status updates and Twitter feeds to deal with. We are living in a mad 24/7 wired world, which is demanding and relentless.

And this is before computers programmed with Artificial Intelligence have started to flex their bits and bytes. Slowly but surely, unseen digits and cyber-networks are inveigling their way into our daily lives and, to an extent, taking them over. As they will, in due course, our working lives too. It seems inevitable that computers running complex algorithms and nifty nano software will be undertaking some of the tasks we once thought only a person with a good education could do. Doctors, lawyers and accountants are all likely to notice the gentle hum of a digital device encroaching on their patch.

Already, we are feeling threatened by this erosion of our liberties and intrusion into our lives. Our best response will be to do the one thing that no computer in the world can manage, which is to bring our imagination to bear. It is by being creative that we are likely to find contentment, purpose, and a place in our digitized age.

In the workplace, creativity will be increasingly highly prized and well remunerated. Which is good. But there's more to it than that. The very act of making and creating is deeply satisfying, life-affirming and rewarding. Yes, it can be infuriating and at times disheartening, but nothing else can make you feel as truly alive and connected to the physical world as bringing your ideas to life. It is, I suppose, the ultimate affirmation of our humanness.

It is an also an important and powerful form of self-expression. Why else would despotic dictators lock up poets, and extremists destroy artifacts? They are frightened by ideas that oppose theirs, and threatened by those who can express them. Creativity matters. Now, perhaps, more than ever.

We live in a world full of urgent problems: climate change, terrorism and poverty, to name but three. We won't resolve them with brawn; they are obstacles we can only overcome by using our brains—when we are thinking like artists and not behaving like animals.

And we are all artists. We just have to believe it. That's what artists do.

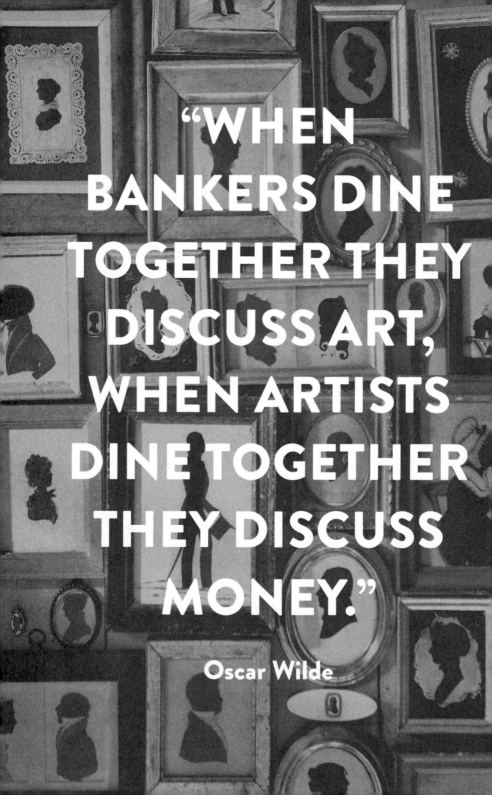

"WHEN BANKERS DINE TOGETHER THEY DISCUSS ART, WHEN ARTISTS DINE TOGETHER THEY DISCUSS MONEY."

Oscar Wilde

1. ARTISTS ARE ENTERPRISING

There are many myths we like to believe about artists. Ours is a romantic view of the painter and the sculptor. To us they represent an ideal. While we toil away at life doing stuff we don't really want to do, in order to put food on the table or because it seems expedient, artists appear to make no such compromises. They follow their own star; do their own thing, regardless of the circumstances, or the consequences. Artists are true and heroic—and necessarily selfish.

They will withdraw into their garret (Seurat), tie themselves to a ship's mast in the middle of a storm (J. M. W. Turner), or walk thousands of miles (Brancusi) in the name of art. Concessions are not made, the motivation is singular: to create a work of worth and meaning. Courage and nobility abound.

Up to a point . . .

In reality, artists are no more courageous or noble or single-minded than the farmers who go to extreme lengths, in extreme weather, to protect their herd. Or a restaurateur who—having waved goodbye to her last customer at midnight—hauls herself out of bed at 4 A.M. the following morning to make sure she's at the market in time to buy the best produce. Or, for that matter, a master bricklayer who has calloused fingers and an aching back from days spent building a house.

Artists are entrepreneurs. They are willing to stake everything for the chance to go it alone.

In terms of dedication to the cause and seriousness of intent, there is little to differentiate between them beyond the way we choose to value their activities. The aim is the same. Which in all cases is neither particularly romantic nor especially high-minded. It is to survive and, with luck, thrive by making enough money to continue doing their thing.

But while farmers and restaurateurs will talk for hours about the practicalities of cash-flows and operating margins, artists tend to remain tight-lipped on the subject of money. It's a bit vulgar, demeaning even. Added to which it risks ruining the illusion we have created that they are deities untouched by the grubby realities of everyday life.

There is the occasional exception, though. Andy Warhol was so fascinated by money and materialism he made them the subject of his work. He called his studio a factory, and once famously said, "Making money is art and working is art and good business is the best art." He made screen-prints of consumer products, celebrities and dollar signs. Warhol actually manufactured images of money that he would then exchange for the real thing. Now, that was good business.

"GOOD BUSINESS IS THE BEST ART."

Andy Warhol

He was extremely enterprising. But then, so are all successful artists. They have to be. Just like the farmer, restaurateur and builder, artists are the CEOs of their own businesses. They need to have an acute sensitivity for marketing and an implicit understanding of brand; ugly corporate concepts they would never mention in polite company but which are actually second nature to them. They wouldn't survive long were they not. After all, they are in the business of supplying products that have no real function or purpose to a wealthy clientele; customers who value brand distinction above all else.

It is no coincidence that the great historical centers of art, such as Venice, Amsterdam and New York, were simultaneously the great global centers of business. The enterprising artist is drawn to money like a graffiti writer to a wall. And that's the way it has always been.

Peter Paul Rubens (1577–1640) was a good artist and a brilliant businessman. While his assistants worked all hours at his studio-cum-factory in Antwerp, the enterprising Rubens would travel to the splendid aristocratic houses and royal courts of Europe and inform their well-heeled owners that if they were to keep up with their peers they would need one of his giant, fleshy, baroque paintings hanging in their Great Hall. Rubens established best practice in the art of door-to-door selling centuries before the Avon Lady had her calling.

Artists are entrepreneurs. They are willing to stake everything for the chance to go it alone and make the work they feel compelled to create. They will beg and borrow to pay the rent on their studio, to buy the necessary materials, and to feed them-

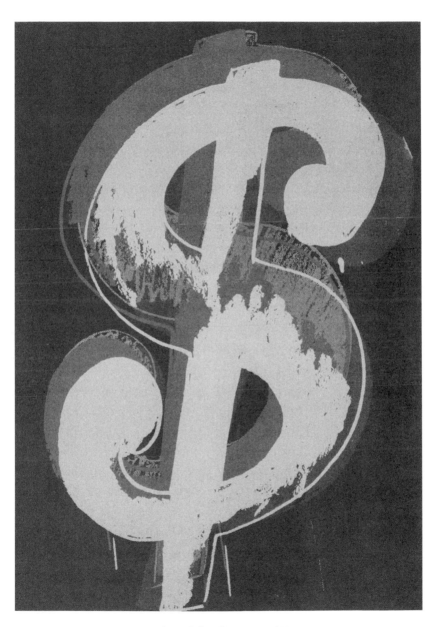

Andy Warhol, *Dollar Sign*, c. 1981

selves during the long months of endeavor. All in the hope that they can sell their artwork at a price that will cover their costs and leave enough (profit) to reinvest in the next piece. With luck it too can be sold, maybe at a slightly higher price. And then, if things go well, a bigger and better studio can be rented, assistants can be hired, a business can be built.

The intellectual and emotional motivation isn't profit, but it is an essential component. Profit buys freedom. Freedom provides time. And time, for an artist, is the most valuable of commodities.

Even Vincent van Gogh, perhaps the most celebrated example of the romanticized bohemian artist, was actually a thoroughly enterprising and commercially aware entrepreneur. He wasn't a destitute pauper, as fable has it, but a start-up businessman who went into partnership with his younger brother Theo, an art dealer.

Theo was the money man. He invested heavily in his older brother, to the extent that expensive canvases and paints were usually readily available for the voracious Vincent (as were accommodation, food and clothes when needed).

Vincent managed this vital source of revenue with all the care and attention one would expect of a small businessman dealing with his bank manager. He sent Theo a constant stream of letters updating him on progress. These would often include a request for further funds, in return for which the painter made plain that he fully accepted his commercial obligations. In one such letter, Vincent said, "It is absolutely my duty to try to make money by my work."

Theirs was a joint investment in a commercial enterprise that you could call "Vincent van Gogh Inc.," which, Vincent reassured Theo, would "earn back all the money you have been lending me for several years." He also understood the need to be flexible and accommodating in business, promising in 1883, "In no case shall I refuse a serious commission, whatever is asked for, to my liking or not, I'll try to do it as required, or do it again if required."

Vincent made the business case to his brother for investment in the most basic language of enterprise: "Look, the canvas I cover is worth more than a blank canvas." He even wrote to Theo with an alternative plan, should the artist business fail: "My dear brother, if I wasn't all washed up, and driven crazy by this bloody painting, what a dealer I'd still make."

"It is absolutely my duty to try to make money by my work."
Vincent van Gogh

That was a bit optimistic. Vincent had already tried his hand as an art dealer and proved to be fairly hopeless. But it does demonstrate his explicitly commercial nature; when the going got tough, Vincent's view was to get out there and sell.

Could it be that Warhol was a line short in that quote about good business being the best art? Might he have concluded the sentence with ". . . and the best artists are good at business," citing the van Gogh brothers as a prime example? Admittedly, their partnership wasn't an immediate commercial success, but had they not both died in their midthirties, before "Vincent van Gogh Inc." had really got going, the chances are they would have enjoyed the fruits of creating what is now one of the world's most famous and desirable fine art brands.

The artist businessman is not an oxymoron. An enterprising outlook is essential for creative success. As Leonardo da Vinci once observed, "It has long since come to my attention that people of accomplishment rarely sat back and let things happen to them. They went out and happened to things." That is the artist's way. To happen to things. To turn nothings into somethings.

They do it by behaving like any other entrepreneur. They are proactive, independent, and so ambitious that they will seek out, not avoid, competition. Which is why any artist worth the name headed to Paris in the early twentieth century. That's where the action was: the clients, the networks, the ideas and the status. It was a cut-throat environment in which most were operating without a financial safety net: a hand-to-mouth existence in a highly competitive environment that had the effect of stimulating their creative impulse.

Artists turn nothings into somethings. They do it by behaving like any other entrepreneur.

For a group of people who are forever protesting that they don't like art competitions, artists sure spend a lot of time taking part in them. You can't move in the art world for prizes with cash attached and biennials dishing out gold medals. They have become an essential step on the career path for any aspiring contemporary artist, a chance to make contacts and build the brand. It's a tried and tested formula, of which one of the most recent beneficiaries is an American artist called Theaster Gates, who won the Cardiff-based Artes Mundi art prize in 2015.

Along with the plaudits and press coverage, Theaster was

presented with a £40,000 winner's check, which he promptly decided to share with the nine other shortlisted artists. This was a very unusual and generous gesture. But then the forty-one-year-old is a very unusual and generous artist. He is part sculptor, part entrepreneur and part social activist. He is the most inspiringly enterprising individual I have ever met.

He was born and raised in Chicago, where he still lives. It's a beautiful city, especially if you live downtown or on the North Side. Theaster lives on the South Side, which is far grittier. It's littered with boarded-up houses, empty lots and kids hanging out on street corners. Unemployment is very high, aspirations are very low, and it can be dangerous. Hundreds of shootings take place there. It has been called the murder capital of America. Around 99.6 percent of people living on the South Side are black, according to Theaster, who says, "If you see a white guy walking around here, he is either looking for crack, is a social worker, or he is an undercover cop."

He describes the South Side as "the bottom": somewhere people only move from, not to. He is the exception proving his own rule, having moved there in 2006 because it was cheap, and just a short walk across Hyde Park to the University of Chicago, where he had a job—and still works—as an arts programmer.

Theaster bought a single-story house at 6918 South Dorchester Avenue, which had once been a sweet shop. He converted one of its small rooms into a pottery studio so he could pursue his hobby of making ceramics. He was drawn to the craft because he liked the notion of taking the lowliest of materials, mud, and transforming it into something beautiful and valued. What started out as a modest sideline would eventually lead to him becoming a major figure in the art world.

At weekends he would take his pots and jugs to county fairs, but he found running a stall upset him. People would haggle over the price of a plate or a mug, pieces of pottery he had made with his hands and his heart. He decided he would rather give them away than have his work demeaned by bartering.

Theaster stopped going to county fairs and decided to try the rarefied air of the art world instead. After all, there were plenty of white potters whose work had been shown in leading galleries and collected by museums. Studio potters like Grayson Perry and Elizabeth Fritsch were a big deal.

> "There's got to be something countering acts of destruction with acts of creation."
> Theaster Gates

In 2007 Theaster mounted an exhibition of his pottery at Chicago's Hyde Park Art Center, to which he added a little twist. He presented the work not as his own, but as being by a legendary Asian ceramicist called Shoji Yamaguchi, who, unbeknownst to all, didn't actually exist.

Shoji Yamaguchi was Theaster's doppelgänger, a fictional character through whom he planned to transform his pottery into art. He concocted the name by combining two of his great influences. Shoji Hamada (1894–1978) was a masterly Japanese studio potter and an important figure in his own country and abroad. Yamaguchi is the region in Japan where Theaster had previously spent a year studying ceramics.

To convince visitors that the plates and bowls displayed

before them were made not by a local, middle-aged African-American man but by an exotic Japanese master, Theaster conceived an elaborate backstory for the fictitious Mr. Yamaguchi. It told of his arrival in America during the 1950s, having been drawn to the United States by the marvelous black clay of Itawamba County, Mississippi. He stayed and married a black woman. In 1991 the then elderly potter took his wife back to Japan to show her where he had been born. The trip ended in tragedy when they were both killed in a car crash.

People liked the show; they admired Shoji Yamaguchi. But that was nothing compared to the strength of the reaction that came with the revelation some time later that the whole conceit was a con. The art world hugged itself with glee. What a wag this Theaster was! What a clever guy! The pots were okay, but wow, what an artist! Theaster Gates, conceptual artist and myth-maker, had arrived. It was the opportunity for which he had waited decades, and now that it had come, this enterprising adopted son of the South Side wasn't about to let it pass him by.

What he has since achieved by leveraging his position as an artist is both impressive and inspiring. He has brought to bear his deep knowledge and passion for the built environment, the religious values of his parents, and his notable intellectual and artistic abilities. To this potent mix he was able to add a natural gift for rhetoric, a hustler's instincts and a missionary's zeal.

He has become a cultural entrepreneur: an artist who is using his position to improve his neighborhood. He is the closest thing the art world has to a Robin Hood figure.

In *Art Review* magazine's 2014 Power 100 list, Theaster

Gates was placed in the top 50, right up there among the über-curators, museum bosses and unimaginably wealthy collectors. His work has been bought by some cool people, and shown in some cool places. And that's astonishing when you consider what he is selling, which is rubbish.

At least that's what it is made from. Theaster's artworks are constructed from the worthless materials he has found in the abandoned buildings in his run-down neighborhood: broken floorboards, chipped concrete pillars and old fire hoses. He dusts them down, polishes them up, and encases them in smart wooden frames with a clean modernist aesthetic. He then sells them for a lot of money. How's that for enterprising?

> "In art, the hand can never execute anything higher than the heart can imagine."
> Ralph Waldo Emerson

What makes his form of artistic enterprise unusual, though, is how he is using the elevated status that art and artists have in our society to try to effect positive change on the South Side. Frankly, he is amazed by the financial value collectors are attributing to his artworks made from rubble and ruin. As reported in the *New Yorker* magazine, he told an audience at the University of Massachusetts that he "couldn't have imagined that a piece of fire hose or an old piece of wood or the roof of a building would have gotten people so wet that they would want to spend hundreds of thousands of dollars on those objects."

But they do. And maybe that's partly because they know what Theaster does with the money he makes. Which is to reinvest it back into renovating the houses from which the materials originally came. This he does with the sort of love and care that was so palpably missing from the properties when he originally found them; the blighted becomes beautiful. You can see this for yourself as you walk down South Dorchester Avenue. Three houses immediately catch your eye.

First, there is 6918 South Dorchester Avenue, which had been Theaster's home and pottery studio, but is now renamed the Listening House, a small cultural center filled with the bankrupt stock of Dr. Wax Records, which went out of business in 2010.

Next is 6916 South Dorchester Avenue, an abandoned property Theaster bought for a few thousand dollars after the 2008 financial crisis. He decorated it with vertical strips of weatherboard and renamed it the Archive House. He has filled it with old copies of *Ebony* magazine, thousands of books from the defunct Prairie Avenue Bookshop, and tens of thousands of glass slides from the Art History department of the University of Chicago.

Finally, there is 6901 South Dorchester Avenue, now Theaster's home. At least the top floor of the building is. The ground floor is a meeting space and cinema to which locals are invited to watch movies and take classes in film production. It too has been renamed and is now known as the Black Cinema House, a third theme-specific cultural center. They are collectively known as the *Dorchester Projects*, a hub of African-American culture that shares a style of renovation. Theaster describes his method of rebuilding as a "gut-rehab," whereby he reactivates neglected properties using the money he has received from selling their derelict interiors to rich fine-art collectors.

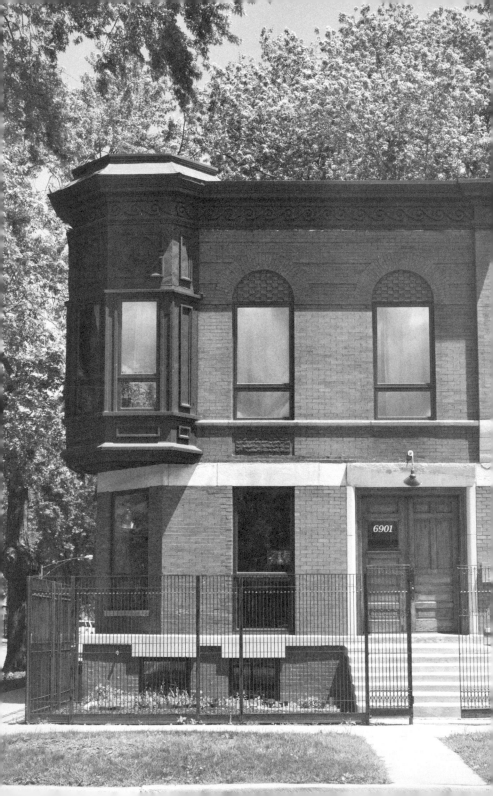

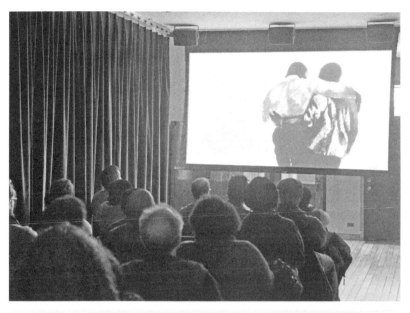

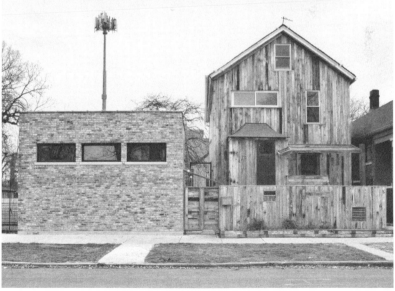

Theaster Gates, *Dorchester Projects*, 2009

For him, the unglamorous, old-fashioned, time-consuming hard work that is required for the rebuild is the part of the process from which he takes the most pleasure. Laboring goes deep with Theaster, who is the ninth child (and only boy) of a teacher mother and a roofer father. He is perplexed by the all-consuming nature of our digital world, particularly the way in which he thinks it has diminished those working in the industrial arts.

> *We have to make labor more skilled and more sensitive, we have got to bring that back. We have to bring dignity back to labour. We have to assume that the entire world will not be a tech-invested world. A skilled hand will create new sectors of opportunity. Because the tech dude doesn't know how to change his plumbing anymore—it's true. I don't think there's a dignity issue in being a plumber. When I watch these guys solder copper I realize that they are much more sophisticated than I am, keeping water out of places you don't want it is a big deal. It's about a man's usefulness. I've watched men and women lose their jobs during economic meltdowns and I've watched men who are no longer able to sustain their families quake. Rational, well-educated, black or white men, lose it, because this thing that gave them dignity was taken away.*

This is the specter that drives Theaster Gates, in terms both of his own life and career, and of those living in his neighborhood. His work is about representing the forsaken, providing an economic and social catalyst for the community, and using his expert knowledge of urban planning to work at the margins of bureaucracy to shift policy, in order to galvanize areas of deprivation by changing public perceptions of a house or a block.

He embodies Warhol's mantra of good business being the best art. Business is Theaster's art, and vice versa. He thinks "an artist's power isn't the ability to monetize a moment, the real power artists have is the capacity to change the world. There's all these people in the world doing horrible acts of destruction—leveling mountain tops, creating wars—there's got to be someone countering these acts of destruction with acts of creation."

We know the art world is a hustle, but it is unusual to have an artist who admits it, and then goes further by openly trading on it. Theaster Gates's art is political, powerful, unflinchingly critical and unashamedly based on leveraging his status as an artist. He has turned the art world hustle into a work of art, which is about as enterprising as it gets.

He now owns a couple of streets, some fancy houses and a massive studio making the furniture and fittings for each building he is renovating. He is interested in the "poetics of materials." How old materials "deserve" a new life because they "stand in for other histories, other people."

Is he now a property developer trading as an artist, or an artist trading as a property developer? It doesn't really matter. If he gets rich from doing up his neighborhood, for being a one-man regeneration scheme—then good luck to him. The point is that he has achieved so much in the name of art. He is presenting a radical new economic model simply by thinking like an artist.

SUCCESS IS VERY OFTEN DOWN TO PLAN B.

2. ARTISTS DON'T FAIL

This chapter is not about failure in a heroic sense, or in a fetishizing kind of way as promoted by the motivational-speaking Fail Better brigade (an expression misleadingly isolated from a despairing Samuel Beckett text). And it is categorically not about how it is good to fail.

No, this is about the real thing that has happened to us all and we wish it hadn't: the embarrassing, debilitating and deeply unpleasant experience of feeling a failure. It is about the days and weeks and years after your project has crashed ingloriously at your feet, leaving you with a crumpled heap of ideas and experiences to sift through for any fragments that might be worth salvaging. It's about the notion of failure in the context of creativity.

Failure is not the same as making a mistake, although a mistake can lead to what at first might appear to be a failure. Nor is it necessarily about being wrong. We learn by our mistakes and making errors, but I'm not so sure we do when we feel like we have failed. That's because it is not always obvious to us when exactly we failed, or what part we played in it. The word appears so categorical and absolute, yet it is surprisingly soft-edged.

Failure is subjective, marginal and mercurial. For years Monet, Manet and Cézanne had their paintings rejected by the all-powerful official Salon in Paris. All three artists were considered failures. But within a few years they were hailed as visionary pioneers whose paintings went on to be considered some of the most important works of art produced in the modern period. Who, then, in hindsight, failed? It would appear the Salon, not the artists. The same goes for exams. The poet John Betjeman went to Oxford University, where he was taught by the writer C. S. Lewis, but failed his degree. As we know, he subsequently wrote some of the twentieth century's most enduring poems. Was he the failure at Oxford or the other way around? Or were both parties? Or neither?

Failure is not the same as making a mistake, although a mistake can lead to what at first might appear to be a failure.

We are dealing with an ambiguous and temporary concept here. But knowing that doesn't help much if your business has recently collapsed, or your soufflé didn't rise, or your first novel has been rejected for the umpteenth time. That is when a sense of failure hurts. It doesn't feel ad hoc or mutable

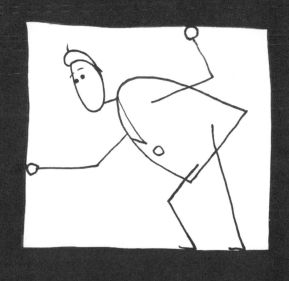

then. It feels rigid and nasty and uncompromising. It feels permanent. And the truth is that there may well be no way back for that business or soufflé or book, but there is for you, and, what's more, that so-called failure is part of the reason why.

When it comes to creativity, failure is as inevitable as it is unavoidable. It is part of the very fabric of making. All artists, regardless of their discipline, aim for perfection—why wouldn't they? But they know perfection is unobtainable. And therefore they have to accept that everything they produce is doomed to be a failure to some degree. As Plato argued, the game is rigged. Which, if you think about it, makes the concept of failure close to meaningless.

The logical conclusion must be that there is no such thing as failure. But there is such a thing as the feeling of failure, which is an inescapable part of any creative process. And it's not nice. But unfortunately it is an essential component. Which is where many of us come unstuck. We don't always appreciate that when we experience a major creative disappointment it is both normal and requisite, and certainly not a sign that we should give up. There is a temptation to believe this is the moment when we have failed as opposed to simply being one of the less pleasant parts in the creative process. Artists don't tend to think that way.

When it comes to creativity, failure is as inevitable as it is unavoidable.

Did Monet, Manet or Cézanne put down their brushes and take up accounting when they were publicly rebuffed? Did John Betjeman cease to write and turn his mind to medicine when he was humiliated? No. They pressed on. Not because they were arrogant or insensitive, but because they were totally committed to their craft. They couldn't help themselves. Even if they were far from competent to begin with.

Thomas Edison knew all about the notion of sticking at it. Did the American inventor of the electric light bulb get it right the first time? No. Nor did he crack it on the second, third or even the thousandth attempt. In fact it took him ten times as many experiments to arrive at a commercially viable product. But at no point did he countenance failure. "I have not failed 10,000 times," he said. "I have not failed once. I have succeeded in proving that those 10,000 ways will not work. When I have eliminated the ways that will not work, I will find the way that will work."

If at first you don't succeed, don't try exactly the same thing again.

If at first you don't succeed, don't try exactly the same thing again. You won't succeed, again. Instead, have a think, evaluate, correct, modify and then try again. Creativity is an iterative process.

A sculptor carves a stone until eventually a form is revealed. Is the only successful strike of the sculptor's chisel the final one that completes the work? Were all the thousands of previous incisions failures? Of course not! Each strike leads to the next. Creating anything of worth takes a while; there is no rush. There is plenty of time for wrong turns, for getting lost; for feeling generally hopeless. The crucial thing is to keep going. Artists appear glamorous and blessedly detached, but in reality they are tenacious grafters: they are the proverbial dogs with bones. They are still out there gnawing away long after most of us would have given up and gone home.

"I PROCEED BY TRIAL AND ERROR."

Bridget Riley

And while they are out there, worrying away, they often discover a hidden truth about the creative process. If you look at the career of any brilliantly innovative individual—entrepreneur, scientist or artist—you are likely to find a surprising common trait. Their success is very often down to a Plan B. That is, the thing they originally set out to do has morphed along the way into something different. Shakespeare was an actor who became a playwright. The Rolling Stones were an R&B cover band until Mick Jagger and Keith Richards started writing their own songs. Leonardo da Vinci marketed himself as an armaments designer, and so on. The list of Plan Bs is long and illustrious. And instructive.

Bridget Riley is about as sure-footed an artist as any I have ever encountered. She knows her mind and methods and produces consistently excellent work within her given style. Which is the making of elegant abstract paintings that explore the relationship between color, form and light. In the 1960s she was a pioneer of the Op Art movement, and has since developed her practice along similar lines but with a broader chromatic range. If you look at the controlled, composed nature of her work it suggests an artistic life that has been one long, happy, self-determining procession from art school to international stardom. But that is not the case. She has had a torrid time.

Talent was never an issue. Her painting *Man with a Red Turban* (1946) (see color section at the back of this book), an early riff on Jan van Eyck's *Man in a Turban* (1433), which she produced as a teenager, is evidence enough of her painterly abilities. She went to art school and became a great admirer of the Impressionists, developing a particular liking for artists for whom color was as much the subject as the subject matter itself—van Gogh being the most obvious example.

This led to an interest in color theory and the Pointillist paintings of Georges Seurat. And then she discovered Cézanne and his belief that an image should have an overall design, into which all the individual elements should fit and relate to one another. The years passed by, she continued to paint, but it wasn't working out. She couldn't find a direction to take, an artistic voice that was hers. She was lost and becoming depressed.

By 1960 she was approaching thirty and was no longer the young, talented student with a bright future, but a maturing artist who was all at sea. She painted *Pink Landscape* (1960) (see color section) during this period, an exercise in exploring Seurat's ideas about color and subject and ways of seeing. It was a perfectly good painting, but not very original. Not what we would call "a Bridget Riley." This is the moment when it very nearly all fell apart for her. Nothing was working, in her art or in her personal life. She must have felt like a failure. She certainly considered quitting.

But she didn't. She continued to work away at her artistic problem. It was, though, time for a fresh start. She had spent the past decade immersed in bright colors, but now her mood was dark. It was time for Plan B.

She covered a canvas in black paint in response to the ending of an intense relationship. It was intended as a message to "a particular person about the nature of things . . . that there were no absolutes, that one could not pretend that black was white." As it turned out, she felt her all-over black painting didn't say anything at all. But perhaps it would if she introduced some of the ideas she had been pursuing for the past decade? Could elements from all those so-called failures now be brought usefully to bear?

There was Cézanne's insistence on coherent design, Seurat's theories of color separation, and van Gogh's stark contrasts. Bridget Riley knew how to achieve these, but she had never tried it in purely abstract terms. She started out once again with the idea of a canvas covered in black paint. But this time she modified it by introducing a white horizontal line two-thirds of the way down. The bottom part of the line remained as straight as a ruler, but she added an asymmetrical wave to the top that gradually increased as it made its way to the outer edges of the painting. The effect was to create three separate, contrasting shapes united by the compositional balance. It was a very simple yet very effective way to express the unequal and dynamic nature of relationships—spatial, formal and human: a tense interaction she reflected in the painting's title, *Kiss* (1961) (see color section).

"In art one is either a plagiarist or a revolutionary."
Paul Gauguin

Bridget Riley had found her way, and for the next six years focused her creative energies on black and white abstract images. As with Edison in the nineteenth century, she could now accept all her previous efforts for what they were: staging posts, not failures.

For those people pursuing a creative goal, life should be treated as a lab. Everything you do feeds into everything you do. The trick is to be able to distinguish between the elements you should keep from a previous work or experience and those you must let go. Bridget Riley had to abandon the one thing she thought most important and appealing about painting—color—in order to make any real progress. It didn't mean color could never feature in her work again, only that at that precise moment in time it was the roadblock.

There is more than that to her breakthrough, though. Or less, I should say. As is so often the case with matters creative, simplification was her answer. Only when Bridget Riley went back to the most basic of basics—a canvas covered in black paint—did she find the necessary clarity to progress. Only then did she discover the most precious and liberating of things: her own artistic voice.

As is so often the case with matters creative, simplification was the answer.

Finding a way to express your personal response to the world around you with a distinct technique and style is not something that generally comes quickly or easily. But once discovered, it provides a platform upon which an entire oeuvre can be built, as the Dutch abstract artist Piet Mondrian proved.

Most of us can spot one of his famous grid paintings from thirty feet away. There are the tell-tale horizontal and vertical black lines that form the squares and rectangles the Dutchman filled with his bold blocks of blue or red or yellow. He spent thirty years of his life producing canvases that were variations on this stripped-down, geometric theme. Mondrian's painterly voice was clear and unambiguously his. But it was his Plan B.

Piet Mondrian, like Bridget Riley, was hovering around the thirty-years-old mark before he found his way. Before that he was producing good but gloomy landscapes and images of gnarly old trees, which very few people would even begin to recognize as the work of the modern Dutch master.

And who would correctly pick out the American painter of *Washington Crossing the Delaware I* (*c.* 1951). It is by an artist who would go on to produce some of the most iconic and recognizable images of the twentieth century, none of which looked anything like this post-Cubist, quasi-Surrealist, Juan Miró–inspired effort.

The artist in question is Roy Lichtenstein, the Pop Art painter, who didn't find his artistic mojo until a decade later when he produced *Look Mickey* (1961), the first of what would become his trademark comic-strip images. So, what happened? How did he come to find such a clear and distinct artistic voice after searching for it for so long? Where did his Plan B come from? Was it by chance?

Yes, to an extent it was. And the same applies to Piet Mondrian, Bridget Riley and the Jagger/Richards songwriting partnership. In all cases the catalyst was an external prompt. With Jagger and Richards it was their manager telling them that the way to make money and to have creative control was to write their own songs. Bridget Riley's came from the break-up of a relationship, Mondrian's from a visit to Pablo Picasso's studio in 1912. For Roy Lichtenstein it has been said the trigger came from his young son challenging him to a competition to find out which one of them could paint the best Mickey Mouse.

I shouldn't imagine any one of them thought these events would lead to such momentous outcomes. But they were alive to the possibility. And that's really important. You know that old trope, "you've got to be in it to win it"—well, the same

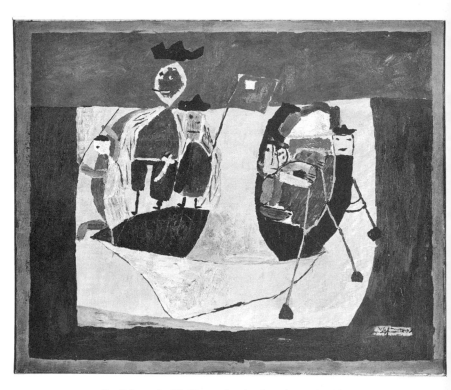

Roy Lichtenstein, *Washington Crossing the Delaware I*, c. 1951

also applies to creativity. As long as you stick at what you are doing, constantly going through the cycle of experimentation, assessment and correction, chances are you will reach the moment when everything falls into place.

Too many of us are either too quick to quit, or, worse, too frightened to even give a new challenge a try in the first place. It seems so risky, the chances of success so slim. But we should remind ourselves that they are non-existent if we don't even give it a go. The way an artist approaches such a situation is slowly and cautiously, learning new skills and gaining insights,

> **"Ideas are like rabbits. You get a couple and learn how to handle them, and pretty soon you have a dozen." John Steinbeck**

so that when it comes to taking the plunge it is an informed risk, and not akin to jumping out of an airplane without a parachute.

It can be difficult to get started. We can feel that we don't have permission to test our talents, whether that's by taking up designing or playwriting. Somehow we are unworthy. Now, in such circumstances I do think we are flirting with failure. A failure of spirit.

To give up before we even start, using low self-esteem or lack of qualifications as an excuse, is, frankly, gutless. As human beings we are all born with not only the wherewithal to be creative, but also the need. We must express ourselves. The only decisions to make are what it is we want to say and through which medium we want to say it. Will it be by building a company, inventing a product, designing a website, developing a vaccine, or painting a picture?

It's a decision that is generally intuitive. We select the activity that appeals and inspires us most: business or baking, design or poetry. After that, it is a matter of plugging away: learning, probing, and being ready for when that unpredictable prompt occurs, precipitating the glorious discovery of finding our own, original artistic voice. And "finding" is the operative word. It is something we already have but that is yet to be discovered and set free.

Roy Lichtenstein wasn't born a pop artist. He wasn't born an artist at all. He had an interest, took some lessons, and got on with it. Nobody gave him permission. You can take a degree in fine art but that doesn't make you an artist. It is not like becoming a doctor or a lawyer—there are no qualifications as such. Vincent van Gogh was basically self-taught, an autodidact

The only decision to make is what we want to say.

as many other artists have been. Does that disqualify him? Hardly. Who is going to stand up in front of all those people gathered around one of his priceless paintings in the van Gogh Museum in Amsterdam and explain to the crowd that he isn't really an artist at all because he doesn't have this qualification or that professional endorsement?

If you call yourself an artist and you make art, then you are an artist. The same applies to being a writer, actor, musician or filmmaker. Sure, there are skills to be developed and knowledge to be gained, but that's all part of the process. There is no passing-out parade or accreditation required. The only person from whom you need permission is yourself. And, of course, that requires a modicum of self-confidence or chutzpah, which can feel uncomfortable. But then, everyone thinks they are a bit of a fraud; you just have to get over it. Take a leaf out of David Ogilvy's book.

The legendary British advertising executive was one of Manhattan's original Mad Men. He set up his eponymous ad agency on Madison Avenue in 1949 when he was thirty-eight years old. He presented himself to the world as a creative genius and the world believed him. But what did he have to back up his claims? A couple of decades' worth of award-winning ads? A roster of clients that was the envy of the Avenue? Proven flair at writing copy? Not a bit of it.

In fact, when David Ogilvy opened his agency he was unemployed. He had no clients or credentials, and absolutely no experience of producing adverts. He did have $6,000 in savings, but that was nothing when it came to competing against big, established New York agencies. And yet, within a very short space of time, Ogilvy's agency was the hottest house in town. He was lauded around the world as an exciting and brilliant creative director. His clients read like a roll-call of the world's most exciting blue-chip businesses: Rolls-Royce, Guinness, Schweppes, American Express, IBM, Shell and the Campbell's Soup Company. To which he added the United States, British, Puerto Rican and French governments.

"Big ideas come from the unconscious. But your unconscious has to be well informed, or your idea will be irrelevant."
David Ogilvy

How did he do it? His initial spur, he wrote in his autobiography, came from remembering "how my father had failed

"IF IT DOESN'T SELL, IT ISN'T CREATIVE."

David Ogilvy

as a farmer and become a successful businessman." Ogilvy Jr. thought he would attempt a similar career move. What followed was a Plan B that required a change even greater and more radical than those made by Riley, Mondrian and Lichtenstein.

Like Betjeman, David Ogilvy had flunked out of Oxford University without a degree. Unlike Betjeman, but in the same vein as George Orwell, he went to work in the kitchen of a large Parisian hotel. He returned home for a spell of door-to-door selling for Aga cooking stoves, after which he was off again, this time to America, where he landed a poorly paid but enlightening job with Dr. George Gallup, the famous pollster. During World War Two he went to work for the British Intelligence Service, stationed in the British Embassy in Washington. And then came the spell as a farmer in Lancaster County, Pennsylvania, where David Ogilvy, his wife and young son lived within the Amish community, tending their hundred-acre smallholding.

Of all these experiences it was the times he spent in the French kitchen, with George Gallup, and among the Amish that shaped him the most. Through the exhausting toils of hotel catering he "acquired the habit of hard work." Dr. Gallup showed him the valuable insights that professionally applied research could provide. The Amish taught him empathy.

Armed with this and a penchant for brevity, he took Manhattan. And London. And Paris. And not by winging it. Well, not entirely. He passionately cared about advertising; he was wholeheartedly committed. He had learned the art of effective communication from selling Agas, and the value of precision in language from sending coded messages during World War Two. He knew hard work was the unsung hero of any creative process. His past had made his future possible: there were no failures, only staging posts.

The unique voice he developed for his work was shaped in those two decades of so-called failure when he was job-hopping and career-changing. He was not one for a pithy one-liner. As an ex-salesman and market researcher he thought advertising was best used as a medium for providing winning information. Consider his classic 1950s press campaign for Rolls-Royce. Yes, there is an image and a catchy headline. But the meat of the piece, the element that made his reputation and built a global business worth hundreds of millions of dollars, is his fabulously terse essay spelling out the product's benefits.

He couldn't have achieved this at twenty-eight. The tone of voice with which he had such enormous success was that of a high-status man with the gravitas of age and experience. He was selling goods to himself. Although he hadn't realized it in those peripatetic years, he was always an ad man. His unconventional training for the job was more useful, and better preparation, than any college course or professional qualification. His working life included time spent as a consumer, service provider, manufacturer and salesman. He had done it all.

And when it came to taking a chance he had the confidence to back himself. He didn't shy away like many of us would have done after years of wandering and wondering. He didn't write himself off as too old or too inexperienced. He didn't fear failure. He was daring and astute. He calculated that his experiences, although unconventional, might be suited to the world of advertising. It was his Big Idea, a notion he spoke about in terms of advertising but that could equally be applied to any creative endeavor.

Yes, artists fail. We all do. But only in the most perfunctory sense, insomuch as not everything we attempt works out as we had hoped. But such instances are never really failures, because through persistence and application we will reach a point of clarity, which is only accessible because of those so-called failures. There we will find our voice, our Plan B, our Big Idea.

A far more important lesson to learn from artists is not that they fail, but that they prevail. Artists make. Artists do.

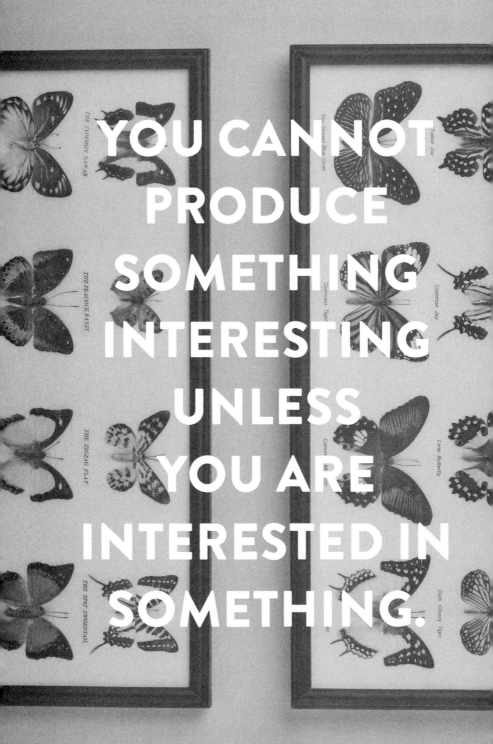

YOU CANNOT PRODUCE SOMETHING INTERESTING UNLESS YOU ARE INTERESTED IN SOMETHING.

3. ARTISTS ARE SERIOUSLY CURIOUS

If necessity is the mother of invention, curiosity is the father. After all, you cannot produce something interesting if you are not interested in something. Outputs need inputs.

But then, curiosity needs a motivation too, a trigger to excite the mind. Our intellectual side doesn't exist in isolation; it's one part of our cognitive being, the other side of which is emotional. It is only when the two are working in tandem that great feats of creativity are likely to be achieved. And that can only really happen when we become passionately interested in something.

It doesn't matter if it's botany or drumming, just as long as the brain has something to focus on in order to harness its powers. I have never met an artist who wasn't a keen student of art, or who didn't enjoy visiting exhibitions, studying the work of peers, and reading prodigiously around the subject.

Passion—enthusiasm if you prefer—is the spur that makes us want to know more. It provides the impulse for the thoughtful inquiry that generates the knowledge, which

fires our imagination to come up with ideas. These lead to the experiments that eventually result in the production of a realized concept. This is the path creativity takes.

It is often a difficult road, full of obstacles and frustrations, but it has the advantage of being open to us all. We can choose to take it at any stage of our lives, even if we are starting the journey from the most unpromising position.

Think of the countless stories of disobedient or disheartened kids at school who were heading for an existence of mediocrity and mayhem, when suddenly their lives were given purpose and meaning after joining a band, or taking up acting, or learning carpentry. Within months, they become experts in their field, reaching a level that would have been considered beyond them. They start making waves instead of trouble, and going from nowhere to somewhere astonishingly quickly, having found an interest that activated their imagination.

The list of famous creative people who were drifting aimlessly before finding a focus for their talents is as long as it is reassuring: John Lennon, Oprah Winfrey, Steve Jobs and Walt Disney spring immediately to mind. And for each one of these celebrated examples there are a thousand less well-

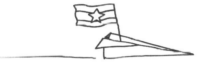

Passion fires our imagination to come up with ideas.

known individuals who discovered an interest that became a preoccupation, which inspired them to produce creations of note.

In all instances it was a deep personal engagement with a particular field of activity that led to something close to an epiphany. To this extent, every artist is seriously curious. But I have never encountered one quite as seriously curious as the Belgrade-born performance artist Marina Abramović, who started out as she meant to go on.

In the summer of 1964, Marina was eighteen years old and living in Tito's Yugoslavia. One sunny afternoon she went for a walk in the park. Having found a suitable spot, she took off her shoes and lay down on the grass and looked up at the blue sky. Moments later, a group of fighter jets roared overhead, trailing thick lines of colored smoke. She was captivated.

The following day, Marina went to the military air base and begged the High Command to fly another section of fighter jets high in the sky "to paint pictures with smoke that will disappear before my eyes." They refused and asked her to leave, telling her she was a silly girl with silly ideas. But they were wrong. She was a curious girl with serious ideas.

Marina wasn't asking for a golden moment to be revived; she was an aspiring artist commissioning a conceptual artwork. She might have come across as a charming but eccentric flaneur, but she was, and remains to this day, a sober, cerebral and dedicated artist interested in new discoveries, world events, ancient history and much else besides. It is her inquiring mind and willingness to treat all experiences as potential sources of inspiration that give her the intellectual raw material with which to create. The same applies to all artists. Curiosity is the immaterial tool that shapes their work just as much as any brush or chisel.

Curiosity is the tool that shapes the work of all artists, just as much as any brush or chisel.

The specific lesson in creativity we can learn from Marina, though, is the innate power and authority her sincerity gives to her artworks. She has spent her career being doubted, lampooned and dismissed, just as Tito's men did back in the 1960s. That she has won out, and is now widely accepted as one of the most influential and important artists of her generation—responsible for bringing performance art into the mainstream in her time, just as Picasso brought modern art to the masses in his—is down to the rigorous approach she has taken to her work. Integrity, she has demonstrated, is impregnable.

Ideas that are born out of ignorance, or which have been flippantly hatched, are invariably weak and most often useless. But those conceived on the basis of real knowledge, inspired by a genuine passion, are much more likely to have plausibility and substance. It is simple, really: our imaginations manufacture concrete concepts when they are set up to do so.

Marina would have been run out of the art world a long time ago if she had not been utterly sincere in her work. After all, she is demanding much more from us than most artists. She is asking us to take a huge leap of faith and be willing to believe that what we are seeing and experiencing in her performance art is more than a piece of theater. We must believe that we are not merely observers, but part of a living, breathing work of art.

Ideas that are born out of ignorance are invariably weak and most often useless.

To convince and cajole a skeptical public to bend to her will takes skill and experience, not to mention courage and confidence. All are essential requirements for any creative undertaking. But they take time to master, and often require the support of a collaborator, as Marina will testify, having spent her formative years working with a German performance artist called Ulay.

They met in 1975 after appearing on the same Dutch TV show. Ulay had arrived looking rather strange. One side of his face was very masculine: head shaved, beard black and eyebrows bushy. The other side was androgynous: clean-shaven, heavily made-up, with his dark hair flowing down over his shoulders. He was half man, half woman, and Marina's kind of guy.

They spent the next few years as nomads, living in a van, washing in gas stations, and performing their peculiar art rituals at fringe festivals and other small venues they happened upon. For Marina, this was an extremely creative and fruitful period. She felt emboldened and energized by having a sympathetic and equally driven ally.

As Albert Einstein discovered through his debating partnership with Niels Bohr, and John Lennon experienced with Paul McCartney, a creative collaborator can be a potent intellectual stimulus, leading to unexpected and otherwise unobtainable discoveries. This was the case with Marina and Ulay.

The work they created in this period has become part of art history. It came out of an intense, shared journey into the boundaries of art and human endurance, which resulted in them testing the limits of their own relationship and personal pain thresholds. This was Marina when she was at her most seriously curious.

For *Breathing In/Breathing Out* (1977), the two artists knelt face-to-face, with their mouths open and locked together, having already blocked their noses with cigarette papers. They began to breathe rhythmically in and out, entirely reliant on each other. After a while, they started to feel faint due to a lack of oxygen and the inhalation of carbon dioxide. They began to rock uncontrollably until they could bear it no longer and fell backwards gasping for air.

In 1980 they created another physically and emotionally

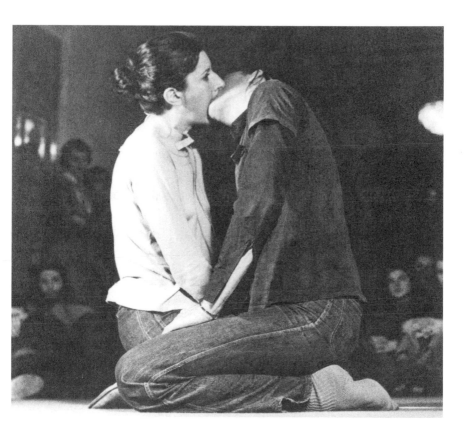

Marina Abramović, Ulay, *Breathing In/Breathing Out*, 1977

extreme work called *Rest Energy*, which once again involved facing each other. But this time there was a bow and arrow between them. The arrow was pointing directly at Marina's heart as she held the front of the bow, while Ulay pulled back the string. They both leaned backwards, counter-balancing themselves by using the taut bow of the now-primed device.

If one of them fell, slipped, or lost concentration, Marina would be dead. To add to the tension they had microphones placed over their hearts, the sound of which was relayed back to them through an earpiece.

Out of context it could appear a melodramatic piece of theater, but then that is part of the illusion of art: nothing is ever exactly as it seems. History has judged these works to be significant; they were not trite ideas hastily made for Marina and Ulay's amusement, but serious investigations into the fragility of life, the inevitability of death and the limits of human trust and pain. They continue to resonate today, both in the art world and beyond, because of the way they were made, which was with seriousness and integrity.

Collaboration can lead to unexpected, or otherwise unobtainable, discoveries.

Each piece required Marina and Ulay to undertake painstaking research into understanding exactly how the body functions, as well as fully comprehending the physics of mass. To this they added years of psychological study. This solid base of knowledge and experience fuelled their inspirations and experimentations, allowing them to conceive original ideas that had power and permanence.

They are not alone in being a seriously curious fine art

double-act whose work has made an international impact. From their studio in London's East End, Gilbert & George have produced an impressive canon of performance art pieces and large-scale photomontages that have changed the nature of sculpture and broken social taboos.

They have an interesting line on the centrality of integrity to creativity. Working on the basis that if you don't take yourself seriously you can't expect anybody else to, they advise: "Make the world to believe in you and to pay heavily for this privilege."

They have. And they continue to do so. Their work has been collected by, and exhibited in, many of the major museums of modern art in the world. They present themselves as Edwardian gentlemen, which is charming until you realize it is actually part of a decades-long performance art project, at which point it starts to feel a little darker and more subversive.

They have described themselves as "living sculptures" when in performance mode, with their bodies the medium through which they explore the subjects that they are interested in. One of which is creativity. In the mid-1990s they enacted a typically staccato, deadpan performance in a work called *The Ten Commandments for Gilbert & George*, a sort of G&G guide to creativity.

It is a good list, tinged with their trademark irony. But I prefer the one compiled by another contemporary art duo interested in creativity as a subject. Fischli/Weiss—as the Swiss art collaborators are known—made a famous video called *The Way Things Go*, which documents a chain reaction where an assortment of inert materials in a studio are nudged

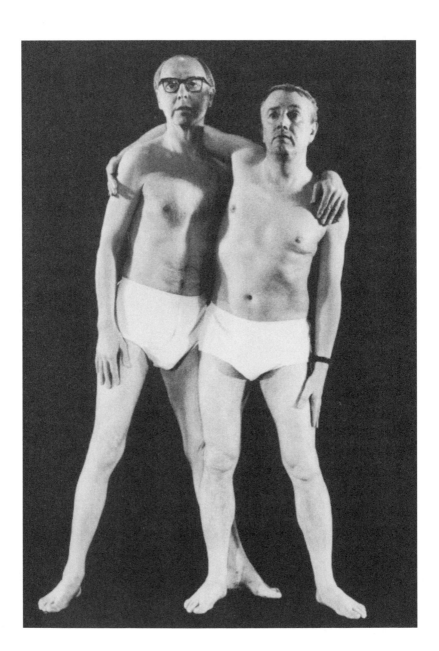

"MAKE THE WORLD TO BELIEVE IN YOU AND TO PAY HEAVILY FOR THIS PRIVILEGE."

Gilbert & George

into movement one by one as each object sequentially collides with another. They were exploring the domino effect, of how one action, or event, affects another. But it was much more about investigating the complexities of the creative process than commenting on the supposed randomness of life. It was a subject they returned to in 1991 with *How to Work Better*, which consisted of a set of instructions—not unlike Gilbert & George's parody of the Ten Commandments—in which they satirized the reductive and banal nature of management speak.

It seems very convincing and reasonable. But something is missing—the one piece of advice that would actually make you work better. Point 9 should not be advising you to "Be Calm," but to "Be Passionate." The reason it doesn't is because passion might cause the bosses trouble.

And you only need to look at a figure such as Caravaggio to realize that a passionate, creative individual is not always easy to manage. Here was a highly emotional artist who lived fast and died young. But in his short time Caravaggio gave the world a masterclass in the art of innovation.

As a character, he had his shortcomings. Most nights he could be found lying face down in Rome's putrid gutters spluttering into his own vomit and blood, having drunk and fought too much. He befriended prostitutes and street hustlers, wielded his sword as frequently as his paintbrush, and spent the latter years of his life on the run for murder.

This is the Caravaggio of folklore: a volatile hell-raiser who happened to be good at painting. It is a compelling and romantic tale that adds notoriety to his work. But it is overblown and even something of a paradox. The reason his art

HOW TO WORK BETTER.

1 DO ONE THING
                    AT A TIME
2 KNOW THE PROBLEM
3 LEARN TO LISTEN
4 LEARN TO ASK
                    QUESTIONS

5 DISTINGUISH SENSE
    FROM NONSENSE

6 ACCEPT CHANGE
                    AS INEVITABLE
7 ADMIT MISTAKES
8 SAY IT SIMPLE
9 BE CALM
10 SMILE

Fischli/Weiss, *How to Work Better*, 1991

has touched millions of people for hundreds of years is not because he was bad, but because he was extremely good.

He was the greatest artist of his epoch. Although only thirty-eight years old when he died, Caravaggio succeeded in dramatically changing the course of art. He released painting from the frigid lifelessness of late Renaissance Mannerism into an age of full-blooded baroque flamboyance. It was a radical feat he achieved by following the conventional creative path.

Passion. That Caravaggio was passionate is beyond doubt; this was a man who wore his heart on both sleeves. But passion needs a focus, and his was art. Having been orphaned as a teenager, the young Michelangelo Merisi da Caravaggio was apprenticed to learn the craft of painting in the studio of Simone Peterzano, a competent but far from brilliant artist who had once been a pupil of Titian. Caravaggio worked hard, developed his basic skills and dedicated himself to finding out what made the old masters so special.

> Caravaggio was a man who wore his heart on both sleeves. But passion needs a focus, and his was art.

Interest. He learned the subtleties of composition from studying Giorgione's paintings, and the way to model the human form from Leonardo's. His interest in the dramatic potential of lighting effects was piqued when he went to look at the early sixteenth-century work of Lorenzo Lotto. And his understanding of gesture almost certainly came from the hours and hours he spent staring up at Masaccio's famous fresco cycle on the walls of the Brancacci Chapel in Florence.

Curiosity. Caravaggio's determination to find an exciting new form of representation in painting led him into the world of lenses. Optics were to society then what the digital age is to us today: a fast-developing technology that was revolutionizing perceptions of the world. With Galileo leading the charge, Italy was a leader in the field.

The intrigued Caravaggio threw himself into learning all he possibly could about the different lenses—convex, biconvex and concave—and what their potential was when applied to his art. It has even been argued by some academics that he painted using a camera obscura as an aid.

Inspiration. Nobody knows the root of Caravaggio's dramatic tendencies, but there is no doubt they were the driving force behind many of the innovations he introduced. His artistic goal was to make paintings that were as shockingly realistic as those being produced by his peers were dull and artificial. Drama was his inspiration, lenses his salvation.

When Caravaggio arrived in Rome in 1592 life was not easy for any unknown artist in what was then the world's art capital. Work was hard to come by, the competition was fierce, and money was in short supply. The cost of buying art materials would have accounted for most of what he earned, leaving him with very little left with which to pay models to sit for him.

Experimentation. Caravaggio found that the solution to his limited funds was surprisingly close at hand. Using the knowledge he had acquired in optical trickery, he simply placed a mirror to his left, set up his easel, primed his canvas, looked into the reflective glass, and . . . there before him was a model who wouldn't cost him a penny: a handsome, twenty-one-year-old Italian called Caravaggio.

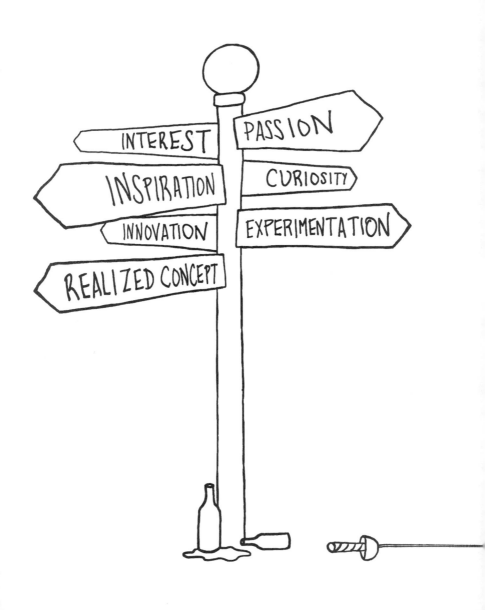

He must have been thrilled by what he saw. Not by his own image, but by the revelation of how optics could transform his art. It seems likely that the *Self Portrait as the Sick Bacchus* (1593) (see color section) is the outcome of his discovery, a painting that is quite different from any other produced at the time. It is so incredibly realistic. And dramatic. The single light source catching the contours of the boy's muscular body is overtly sensual, an erotic theatricality Caravaggio emphasized by setting the figure against a pitch-black background.

This painting heralds a new age in art: an age of expression and movement, color and drama. In this one experimental picture the Baroque era begins.

Innovation. Has there ever been an artist as passionate as Caravaggio? I don't think so. It gave him the power and purpose to successfully challenge orthodoxy at the most orthodox of times.

His temperament clearly played a big part in his art. You can tell from the elaborate style of his compositions, the emotional nature of his storytelling, and the swashbuckling painting technique. But there is another aspect to his work that makes it instantly recognizable and lastingly memorable, representing yet another innovation introduced by the fiery Italian.

It is the accentuating technique he developed for contrasting light and shade for pictorial effect, known as chiaroscuro. Look at any of his famous paintings and you will be immediately struck by the space in which the action appears to take place. The dark background and heavy shadows dramatize what is happening in lighter elements to such a degree that they seem to lift off the surface and come towards you.

Caravaggio's use of chiaroscuro is as startling and fresh now as it was when he first used it over four hundred years ago. You can see its legacy in the films of Orson Welles and Alfred Hitchcock, and the photography of Man Ray and Annie Leibovitz. You could say that Caravaggio was the world's first cinematographer.

Realized concept. Caravaggio had now arrived at the final stage of the creative process, the stage that might seem the least onerous, but is in fact one of the hardest: turning everything he had learned, developed, tried and tested into something concrete and enduring. This is not something that can easily be done alone. Caravaggio needed a partner.

The final stage of the creative process is in fact one of the hardest: turning everything learned, developed, and tested into something concrete.

Marina had Ulay, Gilbert had George; Caravaggio had no one. But he didn't need another artist to work through an idea in the way Picasso and Braque would later join forces to develop Cubism. In fact, he didn't need a creative partner at all. What Caravaggio required was a patron. He needed money.

His creative enabler came in the aristocratic shape of Cardinal Francesco Maria del Monte, the well-connected, art-loving owner of an enormous palazzo in Rome. Although the Cardinal was a high-ranking religious man who counted the Pope among his friends, he immediately took to the rough-edged Caravaggio and his clever innovations. Surprisingly, perhaps, he wasn't at all against the artist's radical realism. Nor did he seem to mind that nobody before had presented Jesus as Caravaggio chose to do in *The Supper at Emmaus* (1601) (see color section). Christ is depicted as a beardless, ordinary-looking man, sharing the main stage of the painting with a bowl of fruit.

Like Marina Abramović, Caravaggio was not happy to simply confront the viewer; he wanted to make us part of the action, a character in the story. As soon as you stand in front of one of Caravaggio's great paintings—such as the grisly *Salome with the Head of John the Baptist* (1607) (see color section)—you become part of the story. To whom is Salome proffering the platter on which John's head is being placed? After a short while it becomes apparent it is you, the viewer!

Caravaggio spent the next fourteen years of his life realizing his concept to lasting effect. The legacy of his creativity has spread across borders, centuries and art forms. The film maker Martin Scorsese credits the artist for the bar scenes in his movie *Mean Streets* (1973), while his baroque chiaroscuro was clearly an inspiration for the late British fashion designer Alexander McQueen. They only discovered his genius because they were just as seriously curious as Caravaggio, Marina and Gilbert & George.

"THERE IS NO NEW THING UNDER THE SUN."

Ecclesiastes 1:9

4. Artists Steal

This is about disruption and how to manufacture ideas. It's about the techniques involved and how we can all set ourselves up to have original thoughts. It is also about recognizing that they don't come out of the ether. Yes, brainwaves happen, but only because we have primed our unconscious to have them.

Ideas emerge from a specific way of thinking.

They come when we encourage our brain to combine (at least) two apparently random elements in a new way, through a mixture of disruption and application. It is an approach that has been identified—among others—by Albert Rothenberg, an American psychiatrist who has spent his professional life studying creativity in humans. He has interviewed and studied numerous leading scientists and writers, and through his research pinpointed specific, consistent forms of cognitive behavior displayed when someone is generating an idea. He calls it homospatial thinking. Rothenberg describes it as "actively conceiving two or more discrete entities occupying the same space, a conception leading to the articulation of new identities." He illustrates his theory with the results of a survey he conducted based on this poetic metaphor: "The road was a rocket of sunlight."

He asked the participants where they thought the poet's inspiration had come from. The majority thought it derived from physical observation. One speculated that the poet had been looking at a road and a shaft of sunlight had appeared in the shape of a rocket. Another that the poet was driving a car on a sunny day and it felt like he or she was traveling in a rocket. Neither guess was correct.

Albert Rothenberg reports that what actually happened was the poet had found the two discrete words "road" and "rocket" appealing. Particularly when they were combined and their sounds, shapes and (in an alliterative sense) relationship worked harmoniously. But how could the poet turn them into a metaphor? When are they actually ever the same or comparable?

This conundrum prompted the poet's unconscious into

action, and a period of free association followed. The word "sunlight" suddenly came to the poet's mind, and with it the notion of sunlight shining on the road. The combinations were made, and an original meta- phor was constructed. The poet had taken two "discrete entities"—road and rocket—forced them into the same conceptual space, and trig- gered a creative process in which the brain goes into problem-solving mode. And problem-solving is all about thinking, and that requires imagination, which is what leads to that moment of inspiration.

Often the "new" element in really big ideas comes in the form of a disruption.

That's how ideas are generated. Unusual combinations, mixing old and new, stimulate original ideas, that is, ideas with origins.

Of course, that doesn't necessarily mean the idea is good or valuable. The quality comes when the idea is focused on a subject in which we are knowledgeable and interested. What is exciting, particularly for those of us who think we are not creative, is the fact that we can all make these types of combinations, which are shaped by our own personality and temperament. Nobody else could possibly make the same connections in the same way; what we conceive is uniquely ours.

Often the "new" element in really big ideas comes in the form of a disruption. Moving home, changing jobs, conflict and heartbreak can all stimulate your brain to start making some radical connections. In our lifetime technology has been a major disrupter, making what was once impossible possible.

"I BEGIN WITH AN IDEA AND THEN IT BECOMES SOMETHING ELSE."

Pablo Picasso

Take, for example, the old idea of an encyclopedia, reapply it to the Internet age and, hey presto! you have Wikipedia.

The same applies to social disruption: what was once impermissible becomes permissible. Take, for instance, the graphic language and sexually explicit scenes in D. H. Lawrence's novel *Lady Chatterley's Lover*. The unabridged version was banned in Britain for over thirty years, until a court case in 1960 resulted in the decision being overruled. Profanities and illicit sex had always been part of life, but now it was finally acceptable to depict them in a literary form. British writers took full advantage of the change by producing ground breaking work, from Philip Larkin's expletive-rich poem "This Be the Verse" to Joe Orton's socially provocative *Entertaining Mr. Sloane*.

Both writers were following in Lawrence's wake. They were, to an extent, copying him. Or, at least, stealing an idea or two. Which is something that always occurs in the creative process but is often underplayed. The French writer Émile Zola once said when musing on art that it was simply a "corner of nature seen through a temperament." In other words, creativity is the presentation of pre-existing elements and ideas filtered through the perceptions and feelings of an individual.

Appropriating someone else's proven ideas is the obvious and inevitable place to start anything. We all know the saying attributed to Picasso: "Good artists copy, great artists steal." The aphorism has become a little tired over time, which is not entirely surprising as it's been around for centuries. Picasso stole the maxim from the great French Enlightenment writer Voltaire, who commented two centuries earlier that "originality is nothing but judicious imitation."

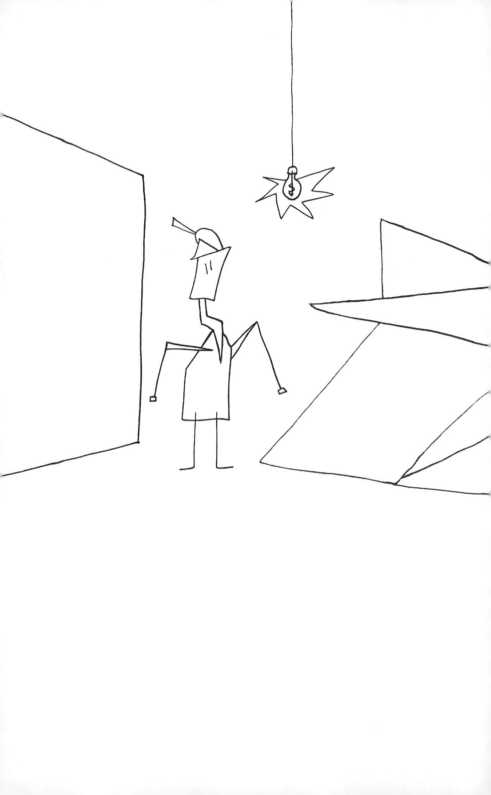

The extensive list of creative geniuses queuing up to confess to intellectual property theft includes Isaac Newton, who said, "If I have seen further it is by standing on the shoulders of giants," and Albert Einstein, who commented that "creativity is knowing how to hide your sources."

The reason these exalted individuals were so keen to credit others was not down to false modesty, or shortness of self-belief, but because it was terribly important to them for us to know. They didn't want to mislead or foster any misplaced notions about creativity. They wanted to disabuse us of any inclination

> "If I have seen further it is by standing on the shoulders of giants."
> Isaac Newton

we might have to take a romantic view of what they had achieved, and to counter the erroneous notion that they were celestial souls blessed with divine inspiration. Both men were brilliant, of course, but perhaps not totally unlike you and me.

They knew that originality in a completely pure form doesn't really exist. They, like us, needed something to react against and respond to, something upon which they could build. Cézanne elegantly summed up this reality when he described the important innovations he had introduced to art with his dual-perspective paintings of the late nineteenth century as simply adding another link to the chain.

Picasso was no different. He too made major breakthroughs in art, most notably with Cubism. Was that an idea he conjured up out of thin air? No. He was just adding the next link in the chain by developing the pioneering work undertaken by the greatest artist of the previous generation, who happened to be a certain Paul Cézanne.

The instinctive reading of Picasso's statement is to conclude that he is making a stark comparison, differentiating between what makes a good artist and what makes a great one. But the statement is subtler than that. He is not describing two opposing philosophies; he is outlining a process. His is an observation on how a person goes from being a good artist to becoming a great one.

Picasso is referring to a journey. He is saying you can't be the latter without first being the former. And to be the former, there is only one place to begin.

Anybody involved in any creative pursuit starts off by copying, be it a ballet dancer or a structural engineer. It is how we learn. Children listen to music and try to play it back note-perfect. Would-be authors read their favorite novels in an attempt to learn a particular style. Painters spend their early years sitting in chilly museums copying masterpieces. It is a form of apprenticeship. You have to imitate before you can emulate.

Look at the early work of any artist and you will see an impersonator yet to find his or her own voice.

It is a transition period, a time for getting the basics right, developing specific techniques, understanding the complexities of a medium, and hopefully for recognizing where the opportunities might lie to add our own link to the chain.

Look at the early work of any artist and you will see an impersonator yet to find his or her own voice. Like a crime scene, there before you is the evidence of the theft of which Picasso speaks. You can identify those masters an artist has copied from and then abandoned, and those he or she has copied from and then stolen. I have seen several surprisingly exposing examples of this, but none more starkly obvious than in an exhibition of some early work by that man from Málaga.

"Becoming Picasso" was a show presented at the small but excellent Courtauld Gallery in central London in 2013. It focused on the year 1901, when Picasso was an unknown yet promising artist. The nineteen-year-old Spanish prodigy had left his home country to make his name among the avant-garde elite of Paris. He had taken his first visit to the French capital the year before, and was returning with high hopes of finding a leading gallery to help launch his career. He was in luck.

A fellow Spaniard who'd been living in France for the past decade had successfully convinced Ambroise Vollard, one of the most important and influential art dealers in the city, to give his young artist friend a solo show. Picasso was thrilled. This was his moment. He packed his paints and brushes and left Madrid for Paris.

Once there he rented a studio on the boulevard de Clichy and began painting. For the next month he did little else, reportedly finishing up to three pictures a day. When he ran out of canvases he painted on wood panels, and when that supply was exhausted he used cardboard. By June 1901 he was ready, with over sixty paintings—some still tacky with wet paint—completed for his first major show at the glamorous Vollard Gallery.

The work he had produced was remarkable. Not because of the quantity or quality, but for the sheer variety of styles.

One moment he was copying his illustrious Spanish predecessors like Goya and Velázquez, the next he was invoking the spirit of El Greco. Two or three paintings later he was clearly imitating the Impressionists and Post-Impressionists. There was *Dwarf Dancer* (see color section), his version of Degas's *Little Dancer*, to which he had added a flamenco twist. Nearby hung *The Blue Room*, the precocious young painter's riff on Cézanne's *Bathers*, and not far from that an image à la Toulouse-Lautrec in both subject and style called *At the Moulin Rouge*. Elsewhere, he had channelled Gauguin's bold outlines and van Gogh's vivid colors and restless brushwork.

This was not a show presenting the virtuosity of an exciting new artist; this was an exhibition promoting a very talented impersonator. I found it a bizarre experience walking through an approximate reconstruction of that Vollard display in the Courtauld Gallery. I hadn't realized Picasso copied on such a grand scale. It was obvious when looking at his brushwork and confidently drawn lines that he was already a good artist, but he certainly wasn't a great one. Dr. Barnaby Wright, the curator of "Becoming Picasso," agreed. He speculated that had Picasso died during the early summer of 1901, when the original exhibition took place, he would have been no more than a footnote in the story of modern art. The fact that he didn't and duly became its single most important figure is thanks to what he achieved in the second half of that year.

The Vollard exhibition had been a success; Picasso had sold several paintings, made some money, and established the beginnings of a market for his work. But he wasn't interested in being a glorified illustrator: he wanted to become Picasso.

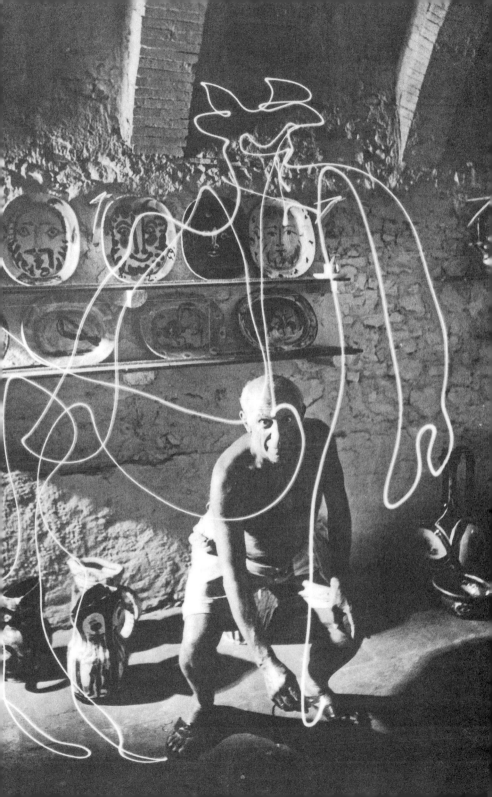

And for that to happen he had to stop producing his bright pastiches, and change tack. He realized it would cause him some short-term financial pain, but hoped it would lead to long-term creative (and commercial) gain. Which is why, with the bold optimism of youth, he stopped copying in July 1901 and started to steal instead.

The difference between the two is vast. Copying requires some skill but zero imagination. No creativity is required, which is why machines are so good at it. Stealing is an altogether different matter. To steal is to possess. And taking possession of something is a much bigger undertaking—the item becomes your responsibility: its future is in your hands.

"Someone may say of me, that I have here only made a nosegay of foreign flowers, having furnished nothing of my own but the thread to tie them." Montaigne

Think, for example, of a stolen car. The thief will inevitably take it in a different direction from the one intended by its previous owner. The same applies to ideas.

And if the ideas in question happen to be in the possession of someone as adventurous, prolific and ingenious as Picasso, the chances are they will be taken on quite a ride. And they were. But first, Picasso had to decide what he wanted to do with the concepts he had pilfered. Where could he take van Gogh's expressionism, Toulouse-Lautrec's subject matter, Degas's bold contours and Gauguin's color blocking?

By July 1901 Picasso was frustrated. He was not only struggling to find his own artistic voice after the Vollard show, but was also still deeply traumatized by the suicide of his great friend Carlos Casagemas, a tragic event that had taken place in Paris earlier in the year. Picasso unwittingly compounded his misery by accepting an invitation to visit the Saint-Lazare women's prison to observe the inmates. What he saw—incarcerated mothers with their young children, women wearing white bonnets to mark them out as suffering from syphilis—left him heavily downcast.

His spirits were low and his temperament subdued. Picasso was still interested in the ideas he had stolen from van Gogh et al, but now they were colliding with an artist who was feeling decidedly blue.

Feeling blue? That was it! Inspiration had struck. He suddenly knew exactly where he wanted to take the innovations of all those great artists from the past. The bold lines, the blocked color and the expressive manner all still had a place, but not in the form employed by his predecessors. He simplified, toned down, merged and cooled. He turned the color dial to blue, and the mood to maudlin.

The transition was remarkable. Picasso had entered what is now known as his Blue Period. *Seated Harlequin* (1901) (see color section) is a very early example. It depicts a contemplative and downcast Harlequin with a white powdered face, wearing a costume of blue and black checkered squares. This is not the typical Harlequin look, which is normally a brightly colored onesie accompanied by a mischievous grin. It is the result of Picasso engaging in a piece of homospatial thinking. He forced a collision between separate entities, by combining two stock characters from the Commedia dell'Arte: Harlequin and the lovelorn clown Pierrot, with his depressed state of mind.

Picasso blended the two identities into one, and by doing so created a third, original figure. The Harlequin in his picture is Casagemas: dead in reality, but still alive in Picasso's mind. He has dressed his dear friend as the male character Harlequin because he traditionally wins the affections of the beautiful Columbine in Commedia dell'Arte. But in real life Casagemas hadn't won his Columbine (hence the suicide), which is why Picasso has combined him with the image of the spurned Pierrot. A blue hue suffuses all.

The more you look at this painting, the more you see how Picasso has incorporated ideas taken from predecessors. We see the beaten countenance of an *Absinthe Drinker* as portrayed by Manet and Degas. There is a glimpse of Gauguin's Tahitian orange, and of van Gogh's *Sunflowers*. Cézanne's contoured *Bathers* are evident in the blue ruffs and tufts of Harlequin's costume. But this is a Picasso painting. The drama and mood are his; the choice and arrangement of combinations are his. But more than that, the style is his.

"It's not where you take things from, it's where you take them to."
Jean-Luc Godard

Walking through the second section of that Courtauld exhibition displaying Picasso's post-June 1901 Blue Period paintings was a revelation. Here was a teenage artist who had gone from a copyist to a master in a month. He had assimilated everything he needed from his heroes, filtered their ideas through his personality and produced a body of work that was at once startlingly original and ingeniously derivative. This was the point at which he started to sign his paintings "Picasso" without the initials and other variants he had previously used. It was the moment Pablo Ruiz y Picasso metamorphosed and became Picasso.

Since which time plenty of people have stolen from Picasso, ranging from the sculptor Henry Moore to Steve Jobs, the co-founder of Apple. Jobs even quoted the "good artists copy ..." line, before going on to say, "We [Apple] have always been shameless about stealing great ideas." Such as Picasso's famous series of illustrations collectively known as *The Bull* (c. 1945). The *New York Times* reported that Apple teaches its stripped-down design ethos to employees by showing them this suite of eleven lithographs by Picasso depicting a bull in an increasingly simplified form.

"I choose a block of marble and chop off whatever I don't need."
Auguste Rodin

Picasso presents the images as a process of reduction—or, as he called it, destruction—to arrive at an essential truth: the essence of a bull. It is an unusual sequence to see, in that he has exposed what normally remains hidden. He has made an image from each stage of a work in progress, demonstrating to us his thought process. The ten lithographs that precede the final version are like a movie director's rushes or an author's edits: the extraneous material that didn't make the final cut.

The series starts with a traditional image in keeping with the etchings of bulls produced by his eighteenth-century compatriot, Francisco Goya. His second effort is fuller and fatter, and seems to be a response to Albrecht Dürer's celebrated *Rhinoceros* (1515). He's still copying at this stage.

By the third version the real Picasso has entered the fray.

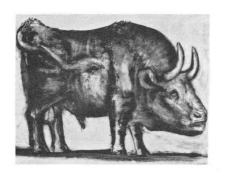

Plate two

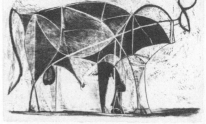

Plate six

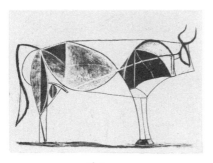

Plate seven

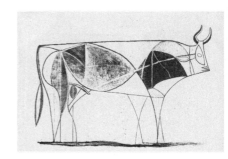

Plate eight

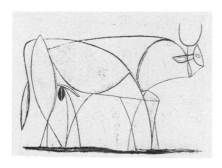

Plate nine

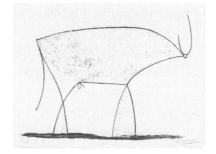

Plate eleven

Pablo Picasso, from *The Bull*, 1945–6

He has started to dissect the animal like a butcher marking out joints. He is taking control, quite literally sizing it up. The fourth plate sees the addition of geometrical lines and a move towards a more Cubist image—he is trying out some old ideas on a lithographic system, which is new to him. The bull's head has turned towards us. The artist is feeling more confident. Versions five, six and seven are reminiscent of a similar series of drawings made by the Dutch modernist Theo Van Doesburg in 1917, as sections of the animal are rearranged to create a more balanced overall design.

Between plates eight and nine we see Picasso realizing that with this particular medium it might be a case of less being more. Matisse was the acknowledged master of line; here Picasso takes his gloves off and challenges his rival on his own terms. Out goes any blocking; from this point on it was about the purity of drawing.

The tenth image shows the artist falling back on experience. The animal's horns have changed from being instantly recognizable to something more akin to a pitchfork, a linear shorthand Picasso had established three years earlier with his *Bull's Head* (1942), made from a bicycle saddle and handlebars. This bull's now tiny head is announced by an enlarged eye, a graphic trick he had been practising since *Les Demoiselles d'Avignon* (1907).

And then, in the final image, everything comes together. A unique picture made by combining prehistoric cave paintings with modern abstraction, an experienced hand with a new process. He had taken ideas from others, and re-used many of his own. He had reacted to Matisse and responded to world events. He had combined external factors with his own memory and disrupted them through learning a new technique. All of which he had distilled through his temperament and instinct to make a highly original work.

Picasso is showing us that creativity isn't about making additions; it is about making subtractions. Ideas need honing, simplifying and focusing. This is a message I assume Apple is keen to convey to its designers: cooks reduce to increase flavor; artists eliminate to achieve clarity.

Picasso's lithograph series is showing us not only how an idea—literally—takes shape, but also where it comes from in the first place. In Picasso's final, simple figure of a bull resides the key to creativity.

It is to be found in the exceptional human capacity to synthesize our experiences, influences, knowledge and feelings into one, unified, original entity. To have such an in-built facility that enables us to make seemingly random connections across a broad range of inputs is marvelous. It has to be the single most important creative faculty we have, as Einstein observed when he said, "Combinatory play seems to be the essential feature in productive thought."

The process our conscious and unconscious selves go through when editing, connecting and combining all that we know and feel into an original coherent thought happens over a period of time. It cannot be forced. It happens when we are awake and when we are asleep. It happens when we are thinking about something else entirely, or playing a game of tennis. It happens because a stimulus in our immediate surroundings—usually without our knowing or subsequent acknowledgement—has alerted our brain to make a connection, which has resulted in a combination being formed that joins all the dots into a perfectly realized, logically robust idea. What feels like divine inspiration is actually instinct.

And few knew this better than Picasso, who once said, "Art is not the application of a canon of beauty but what the instinct and the brain can conceive beyond any canon." He understood the creative power of human instinct, recognized it was a friend to be trusted, not doubted. He openly demonstrates this by working his way through the vast variety of contributing factors in the *Bull* lithographs, presenting us with a Darwinian lesson where only the strongest combinations of ideas survive.

The Bull is not an example of beautiful simplicity: it is the visual manifestation of an exhausting month-long conflict in which Picasso crashed disparate ideas together in order to create new connections. He destroyed the weak, and disrupted the past. In that regard it can be read as a violent image made at the end of World War Two, a very violent time.

There is no such thing as a wholly original idea. But there is such a thing as unique combinations.

But then, creativity is a surprisingly violent act. There is no creation without destruction. And there's no such thing as a wholly original idea. But there is such a thing as unique combinations, which take place in the mind's eye and often start with two or three unconnected mental images that seem somehow pleasing when aligned—the rest, as Picasso ably demonstrated, is hard work.

CREATIVITY ISN'T ABOUT WHAT SOMEBODY ELSE THINKS; IT IS ABOUT WHAT YOU THINK.

5. ARTISTS ARE SKEPTICS

Regardless of the form it takes, creativity can only start in one place. It doesn't matter whether you are planning to bake a birthday cake or designing a fancy new piece of software, there is only one possible way of kick-starting the creative process, and that is by asking a question. What ingredients should I use? How can I make the interface more intuitive?

Take the sculptor who carves away at a block of marble until a recognizable figure emerges. Each tiny incision made by the artist's chisel is a question being asked. What happens if I chip this bit off? Will it shape the torso in the way I want? And that leads to another question: did it work? The final form is the culmination of hundreds, if not thousands, of similar inquiries, followed by decisions, which often lead to more questions and revisions.

Creativity is a constant process of call and response taking place inside our heads. If all is going well, the question–answer routine is like the two sides of our brain working together as if in an inner-cranial pas de deux.

Left Side: *What sort of birthday cake should I make?*
Right Side: *Chocolate sponge topped with white icing.*
Left Side: *Great idea, Right Side.*

More often than not, though, the process is protracted, frustrating and goes more like this:

Left Side: *What sort of birthday cake should I make?*
Right Side: *I can't talk to you now, I'm texting.*
Left Side: *But it's important, I've only got twenty minutes.*
Right Side: *Oh, I don't know. What about a Battenberg cake?*
Left Side: *Too difficult.*
Right Side: *Argh! I didn't mean to press send. What? You? Still? Look, I'll have a think and let you know when you're in the shower . . . in about a month's time.*

The question is then parked in our unconscious, where it stays until a seemingly random trigger provides the spark that connects a few million neurons in our brain, at which point a fully formed answer is provided, as if by magic. It's quite possible you'll be in the shower when it happens.

The American author Edgar Allan Poe wrote a good essay on the essential role that constantly asking oneself questions plays in the creative process. "The Philosophy of Composition" is his personal step-by-step guide to how he wrote his famously macabre poem *The Raven*.

The essay opens with the author debunking the notion that creativity is in any way an act of divine inspiration, stating categorically that at no point was his work the result of "accident or intuition." Instead, he says, it "proceeded to its completion with the precision and rigid consequence of a mathematical problem."

He then describes in a wonderfully superior tone the questions he posed himself and how he subsequently arrived at each of his decisions. He talks in drily practical terms about how he finally decided on a length of 108 lines for his poem, having thought long and hard about the issue:

> *If any literary work is too long to be read at one sitting, we must be content to dispense with the immensely important effect derivable from unity of impression—for, if two sittings be required, the affairs of the world interfere, and everything like totality is at once destroyed . . . It appears evident, then, that there is a distinct limit, as regards length, to all works of literary art—the limit of a single sitting.*

With the scale confirmed in his mind, he goes on to worry about the ultimate point of a poem, which he concludes is not beauty itself, but the contemplation of beauty, because that is what gives us the most intense pleasure. He then reasons that if beauty "in its supreme development, invariably excites the sensitive soul to tears," "melancholy is thus the most legitimate of all poetical tones."

And so, within the first few paragraphs, he has shown how a questioning technique had determined "the length, the province, and the tone" of his poem. The essay then goes into greater and greater detailed analysis of the many other questions he faced and how he resolved them. It is a fascinating read, and still very relevant. The process Poe describes is just the same as the one the film director J. J. Abrams told me he went through when he was working on his first *Star Trek* movie.

I had asked him if he was worried about not meeting the expectations of all the millions of devoted *Star Trek* fans. "Not at all," he said, without missing a beat. What was worrying him and his team, though, was how to move Captain Kirk from one part of the USS *Enterprise* to another. What would be the character's motivation? And how could drama be created out of the situation? An argument with Spock, perhaps? But how to move the Vulcan into place? And what would they disagree about? Or maybe it shouldn't be an argument with Spock at all, but with someone else? Scotty? But why? And so it went on, until they finally had a finished shooting script.

Poe and Abrams were employing a system of logic for honing and proving concepts that has been around for thousands of years. The person with whom we most associate the technique is the ancient Greek philosopher Socrates (*c.* 470–399 BC). He thought that his fellow countrymen took far too much for granted, idly making assumptions instead of engaging their brains. He concluded that it was neither healthy for them nor for society; they were all at risk of living a lie by treating widely held opinions as facts. So he developed a style of open-ended inquiry that would expose weaknesses in suppositions and stimulate Athenian minds to perform at a greater intellectual and creative capacity.

His technique, known today as the Socratic method, is based on assuming nothing and questioning everything in pursuit of absolute truths. Socrates used doubt in the form of skepticism to challenge preconceptions. It is categorically not about cynicism, which is the polar opposite. Cynicism is reductive and destructive and premeditated; skepticism, on the other hand, when intelligently deployed, is enlightening.

It solves problems. And problems—that is, questions in need of a solution—are at the heart of creativity because they force us to think. And it is when we think that we start to question, and to question is to imagine. And to imagine is to conceive ideas, and conceiving ideas is the basis for creativity.

But then, having an idea is easy; it is having a good idea that is difficult. They are the precious jewels that emerge only when we really put our thinking to the test, by subjecting it to the Socratic method.

Socrates famously said, "The unexamined life is not worth living." Paraphrased and reapplied to the creative process it could read: "The unexamined idea is not worth realizing." That is why J. J. Abrams wasn't interested in second-guessing those millions of *Star Trek* fans; not because he was being arrogant or didn't care, but the reverse. He wanted to give them his very best artistic effort. And that meant taking the responsibility for thinking through each and every action.

Because creativity isn't about what somebody else thinks; it is about what you—the creator—think.

And that is why the Socratic method is such a useful tool. It forces us into the all-important act of critical thinking, of thinking for ourselves. Nothing is taken for granted; nothing goes unquestioned. It will expose every contradiction and every fallacy. It will make sure our ideas are based on solid logic and not flimsy presumptions; it can be the difference between making something worthwhile and something worthless.

So potent is it in giving us the ability to think independently that the leaders of ancient Athens became very uneasy with Socrates and his method. They felt threatened, fearing his ways could lead to a civil uprising against them. Protecting their own interests, they concocted some tenuous charges against him, accusing the wise but eccentric old man of impiety and corrupting young Greek minds. Finally, without any recourse to the Socratic method, they found him guilty and sentenced him to death.

Over two millennia later the great neo-classical French artist Jacques-Louis David (1748–1825) painted a famous picture depicting the moment before Socrates's demise. *The Death of Socrates* (1787) (see color section) shows the father of Western philosophy sitting on the edge of his deathbed, bare-chested and as passionate as ever, with his left hand raised, finger pointing to heaven, challenging the opinions of those gathered attentively around him. Meanwhile, his right hand stretches out to grab the deadly cup of hemlock that he has been ordered to drink. At the foot of the bed sits his star pupil, Plato, head bowed and unable to watch the proceedings. Everybody is distraught except Socrates.

It is a large painting, nearly six and a half feet wide and more than four feet tall. But it is not the scale, or David's astonishing skill, that amazes me, nor is it the realization that such a magnificent painting would have involved the artist asking himself thousands of Socratic questions. No, what is staggering about David, about anybody producing a major creative work, is the sheer number of decisions he had to make.

Decision-making is the tortuous by-product of the Socratic method. Because at some point skepticism and questioning have to give way to personal judgment in the shape of a decision made. And that is the most daunting part of a forbidding process. As Socrates knew only too well, the more you question the more you realize that there are no concrete answers. Doubt reigns supreme, an inescapable truth he succinctly expressed when he said, "All I know is that I know nothing."

"The most terrible obstacles are such as nobody can see except oneself."
George Eliot

There's not much about the Socratic method, and by association creativity, that is easy. It is not simply about asking questions; they have to be the most revealing and pertinent questions. And the answers have to be the ones that you feel come closest to solving the problem. But you can never be sure. Which is why artists, authors, inventors and research scientists—in fact anybody innovating—are almost always prone to feeling nervous and vulnerable when presenting their work. However confident some may appear, nobody is ever quite sure. There is always the nagging doubt at the back of their minds that they might have made the wrong call. They all seek reassurance, even if they say they don't.

It is into this quagmire of ambiguity that we all must jump if we want to take advantage of our own capacity for creativity. It is then up to us to try and make certain the uncertain, to make those difficult decisions. Some of our choices will turn out to be correct, some won't. There are times when we will have taken the wrong fork in the road and will need to double back. But that's okay. We are not computers and there are no absolutes in creativity, just educated guesses, but at least they are our own educated guesses, which gives our work its individuality and soul.

As for the days, months and sometimes years of agonizing that we endure to realize our creations, these will disappear from our memories and only be perceptible to the most astute in our finished work. Beneath the superficial perfection of David's *The Death of Socrates* lies an unseen story of torment, of trial and error, of frustration and resignation. We are shielded from all of that; we only see the final decisions David made, and perhaps assume it came easily to the gifted painter. But, as Socrates would have been quick to point out, that is lazy supposition, creativity's number one enemy.

Although the questioning never ceases in the course of creating, some answers are ready-made and supplied by those who have gone before. This is how an apprentice becomes a master, and an artist of any type becomes more skillful. They learn from others in order to be able to take on new and more complex problems as they progress.

Eventually, the dedicated and determined among us will reach uncharted territory, the point in our chosen speciality where there are no longer precedents to guide us, or old hands to advise. The questions we find ourselves asking are new, the answers we have to originate. Which takes us back to Socrates and his method.

It is almost incomprehensible to think that the extraordinary intellectual and creative achievements of the ancient Greeks and Romans were lost for nearly two thousand years. It is said they only resurfaced in the late fourteenth century through the uncovering of old texts and archaeological research in Italy. That rediscovery of the ancients' glorious artistic and enlightened past led to a fundamental rethinking of man's life and place on earth. The questions being asked were so big that the very assumptions on which Western society was based were being reassessed.

Were some of the superstitions and beliefs of medieval culture wrong? Could the individual exist as an independently minded, sentient being able to act without considering spiritual interventions and ramifications? Might it be possible to make discoveries and advances by using only reason and not prayer?

These were the kinds of questions that caused Socrates so much trouble, and those who dared ask them all this time later also had to be wary. But gradually the appetite to explore his culture, ideas and arguments grew, and the Renaissance began. It started most visibly with architecture. The Gothic style of pointed arches and elaborate styling, which had been popular for around three centuries, went out of favour. In its place came the classical lines, simple geometric designs and elegant columns that gave the ancient buildings of Athens and Rome their understated grandeur.

The change in attitude prompted an incredible period of creativity, not unlike our own. We too are in the middle of a renaissance brought about by the discovery of new ways to share knowledge and ideas. The architect behind our Internet-inspired epoch is the computer scientist Sir Tim Berners-Lee. His opposite number back in late medieval Italy was a Florentine architect called Filippo Brunelleschi (1377–1446), who was responsible for placing the magnificent dome on top of Florence's cathedral.

It was a feat of engineering made possible by his extensive knowledge of mathematics, which he used to calculate infinitesimal technical details. Like J. J. Abrams, Brunelleschi believed that using logic was the best way to produce concepts that were functional as well as aesthetically pleasing. To which end he formulated a new way of making architectural drawings that would highlight problems and questions before building had begun. It enabled him to accurately represent three-dimensional objects on a two-dimensional piece of paper by identifying a single vanishing point on the horizon, towards which all lines alluding to a third dimension would recede and converge.

Mathematical or linear perspective, as it is now called, became one of the pillars of the Renaissance. It made the art of Leonardo, Michelangelo and Raphael possible. But only because they were lucky enough to have had a forerunner who did much of the hard work for them by applying Brunelleschi's architectural system to the painted canvas. His name was Piero della Francesca (*c.* 1415–92).

Born into a wealthy family from a prosperous town at the intersection between the Marches, Tuscany and Umbria, Piero della Francesca was initially a specialist mathematician, a subject at which he excelled. But as he neared his twentieth birthday he decided to take up painting. Now if ever there was a moment to be an artist with a flair for math, it was in Italy during the first half of the fifteenth century.

Piero set himself the task of rethinking how the world should be represented in a painting, given the invention of mathematical perspective. It was a challenge akin to the Impressionists reinventing painting in light of the advent of photography. Except Piero was working alone. And if his mission wasn't already difficult enough, he compounded the problem by trying to incorporate the philosophical question of how to reflect society's increasingly egocentric view of life.

> **"A work of art is the unique result of a unique temperament."**
> **Oscar Wilde**

To achieve this in his paintings Piero would not only have to successfully represent three dimensions, but also reflect how man experienced his three-dimensional world. Unlike the art of his medieval predecessors, Piero's paintings would have to have a human, not a celestial, point of view.

It was a creative path fraught with difficulties and blind alleyways, for which only the best navigational aid would suffice. Dante had Virgil as his guide, Piero chose Socrates. He made the commitment to question everything afresh. All assumptions had to be challenged, starting with first principles. Such as, what should be the compositional device in which to set the narrative of a modern painting?

This had not been much of a problem before Brunelleschi's introduction of mathematical perspective, when an artist would generally use a simple two-dimensional background, often consisting of nothing more than one block of color. But that was no way to represent a three-dimensional world that would convince the viewer. Piero concluded that architecture had to provide the framework for his new visual language.

He began constructing pictures around a built environment based on Brunelleschi's neo-classical building designs. Their inherent geometrical nature provided the perfect linear framework to design a stage upon which a pictorial story could take place. It also had the benefit of offering an inherently human-centric view of the world, as the age demanded. Piero was on his way, thanks to the great minds of antiquity: Euclid for his pioneering theories in geometry, and Socrates for his relentless system of inquiry.

There is no painting by Piero that better illustrates his own pioneering work than the *Flagellation of Christ* (1458–60) (see color section). It is said that his rendering of the architectural elements of this painting are so precise that they could be used to build exactly what you see, without recourse to modifications—right down to that staircase in the background. This is mathematical perspective executed to perfection. You could while away hours with a set-square, protractor and compass following how Piero applied Brunelleschi's geometrical principles.

The focus of Piero's complex composition is Christ, although it doesn't appear that way at first. The vanishing point is in the center, just to the right of the flagellator dressed in the green toga, around hip height. Piero has left absolutely

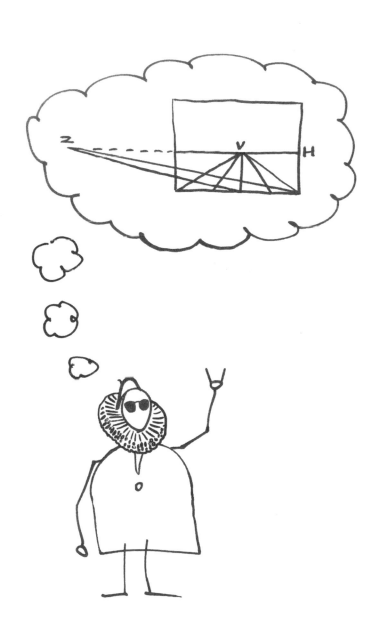

nothing to chance: balance and cohesion were paramount. Every single detail has been assiduously thought through; he has interrogated every aspect.

And there was plenty to consider, not least how to paint people. In medieval art paintings tended to present flat images, letting artists off the hook when it came to depicting volume. But the illusionistic requirements of mathematical perspective meant an artist had to find a way of modeling a person or object in a manner that suggested depth and mass. If he failed, his whole architectural environment would be hopelessly undermined. It is at this point that Piero's genius moves from mathematical mastery to painterly prowess.

After months of speculating, experimenting, making mistakes and reflecting, he found his answer to this fundamental question. It came in the form of two simple five-letter words: light and shade. With the judicious use of both, he discovered he could represent volume authentically. Look at the man standing in the middle of the three figures positioned to the right and in the foreground of the *Flagellation of Christ*. Piero has used highlights and deep shading with such finesse to credibly suggest that the red tunic is covering a three-dimensional figure. He has then emphasized the effect by wrapping the garment around the contours of the man's body, giving us a sense of bulk that is entirely convincing.

It was a promising start, but it only partially solved the problem. There was more work to do. For instance, how could he seamlessly blend his newly volumetric figures into his modern three-dimensional landscape? Brunelleschi's linear perspective worked when it came to portraying a sense of space between people, as can be seen by the relationship in size between the three figures in the foreground and Christ and his tormentors. But it didn't help when it came to blending them all together.

The solution came to Piero with a neat piece of counter-intuitive thinking. True to Socrates, he rejected the impulse to assume, and instead challenged his own assumptions. If light and shade was the answer to creating a sense of volume, then might it also be the way to do the opposite, to present empty space?

Look again at the *Flagellation of Christ* and you can see how he has used light and shade to create a sense of depth. It is particularly obvious to the right of the picture, where the three figures stand in the foreground. The light source is high above their heads, just to the left, as revealed by their shadows. Behind them the roof of the open portico throws a shadow on to the red-tiled pavement of the piazza. Beyond the portico's shadow a light is once again visible, suggesting that there is no building immediately behind it. But our eyes' journey into the distance is not finished. We then reach a two-story building with horizontal black inlays that has an accompanying shadow to its right. Only then do we arrive at the back wall, behind which, in the middle distance, is a tree. The light from the bright sky radiating behind it conveys the impression of open countryside beyond, completing the optical illusion.

"So vast is art, so narrow human wit."
Alexander Pope

The fact that Piero produced a painting with so much meaning and power that art historians are still arguing over some of its elements today is testament to his incredible intellectual ability. Like Socrates, he realized that the more you questioned the less sure you became. Unforeseen possibilities, permutations, contradictions and misjudgments present themselves. Nothing is certain. It's hard. But it is within this mental maelstrom that an artist has to make decisions.

There is, though, some gain to compensate for the pain. The decisions have the validity of being conscious choices derived from an exacting investigation. And that gives a work a perceptible authority and robustness. Thoughtfulness transmits.

Questioning does not make creativity more difficult. Rather it brings clarity and brevity and purity to our ideas.

Piero's work is so considered and so conceptual that it invites the viewer into a Socratic dialogue. The more we look, the more we question. Here we are, over five hundred years later, still scratching our heads about exactly who or what is being portrayed. Which is some achievement when you consider that the real star of the painting is not the people, or the buildings, but the empty space.

In the two-dimensional world of medieval art, space wasn't a problem. In approximate terms, one simply kept adding elements to a picture until there wasn't any room left on the surface. But for the illusion of mathematical perspective to succeed, a sense of space was essential. In fact, the greater the sense of space, the better the illusion. Here was another problem for Piero to solve.

Once more he went through a period of experimentation, before arriving at a solution. Again, it was counter-intuitive. The natural assumption might be that a three-dimensional painting would require more elements to fill the extra "space" created by a receding landscape. But Piero took the opposing view. Rather than adding elements to his paintings, he had a clear-out. He took what we would call today a minimalist approach: the clutter had to go. Less was more in Piero's three-dimensional world.

The *Flagellation of Christ*, as with many of his paintings, is stripped down, containing only the bare essentials. Harmony and beauty reign supreme, a feeling that he reinforces with his finely applied, almost invisible brushstrokes and subtle gradations of tone and color. The effect is to create a scene that is sober almost to the point of being clinical, where the light filling the vast voids becomes the dominant atmospheric force. This is the true brilliance of Piero. He convincingly painted air: the ultimate illusion.

And in doing so he demonstrated that the Socratic process of questioning is not designed to make creativity more difficult and complicated, but the reverse: to bring clarity and brevity and purity to our ideas.

"THERE IS NOTHING WORSE THAN A SHARP IMAGE OF A FUZZY CONCEPT."

Ansel Adams

6. ARTISTS THINK BIG PICTURE AND FINE DETAIL

Right. It's time to get down to the nitty-gritty. To get stuck into the practicalities of making, and what it takes. We're not talking about generalities, such as how much hard work is required, or the benefits of building a team around you, which are universal factors in doing well at most things, creative or not.

We're talking about a very specific mind-set that is crucial when it comes to the act of creating. It is an attitude that can be encapsulated in a simple but demanding rule: always think both big picture and fine detail.

It's something that comes naturally to any experienced artist, no matter the field. I saw a good example of it being put into practice a few years ago when I walked into London's vast O2 arena shortly before a major pop music awards ceremony was due to take place. I was wandering around, searching for the press office, and not having much luck. I felt like Alice at the bottom of the rabbit hole before she entered Wonderland, lost and surrounded by doors. Except there wasn't a bottle labelled "Drink Me"; but there was a "No Entry" sign, which I read as an invitation.

I opened the door, went in and, like Alice, suddenly felt very small. There I was, a solitary figure, standing in the venue's mighty auditorium. Moments later four tiny figures appeared from the back of the huge stage. I didn't recognize the three breaking away towards a bank of free-standing microphones. But I had seen the one striding up the center of the stage before. Not in real life like this, but in newspapers and on the television. She stopped a few feet short of the platform's edge, raised the mic to her mouth, and sang the opening lines to "Rolling in the Deep."

Spend too much time on the fine detail and you will get lost. But if you only think about the big picture you won't create or connect to anything.

What a voice. What a presence. There is a reason Adele is one of the world's favorite vocalists. There she was in this cold, cavernous auditorium, singing her power ballad with all the heartfelt intimacy of Romeo secretly wooing Juliet. She was at once a stadium performer and nightclub chanteuse, filling the enormous space as if it were a room above a pub. Here was an artist delivering the big picture while focusing on the small detail.

It is not as easy as Adele made it look. It requires your mind to constantly go back and forth, one moment concerned with the minutiae, the next stepping away and seeing the broader context. Spend too much time on the fine detail and you will get lost. But if you only think about the big picture you won't create or connect to anything. The two have to work together in sync. If they separate, disaster strikes.

Think of all the city skylines around the world that have been tainted by architects and property developers who have only considered the plot of land on which they are building, without giving enough thought to the surrounding area. London is a prime example. It is a city increasingly full of incongruous, corporate buildings that have been crowbarred into once-elegant Georgian streets and charismatic Victorian wharves.

Creativity, like society, thrives when the individual elements fit within a bigger picture.

It didn't have to be that way. I live in Oxford. It is home to a lot of exceptional architecture, some of which dates back to the medieval period. But it also boasts plenty of fine modern buildings that have been sympathetically designed not only to fit in with their illustrious neighbors, but in some cases to enhance them. Giles Gilbert Scott's broad-shouldered modernist library, which nods across the street to Christopher Wren's neo-classical concert hall, is a good example. And Arne Jacobsen's 1960s ultra-modern scheme for St Catherine's College is to my mind one of the finest buildings in the historic city.

"AN ARTWORK SHOULD POINT IN MORE THAN ONE DIRECTION."

Luc Tuymans

Creativity, like society, thrives when the individual elements fit within, and add to, a bigger picture. Ernest Hemingway would sometimes spend hours on a single sentence. Not because he was attempting to write the perfect solitary line of text, but because he was trying to make that single sentence successfully link to the one preceding it and seamlessly lead on to the next—while also contributing something to the story. He was thinking big picture and fine detail.

One tiny dab of color can radically change the appearance of the largest of paintings.

As do artists. Most obviously, I suppose, those making paintings, where an eye and an ear for both the major and the minor are prerequisites. One tiny dab of color can radically change the appearance of the largest of paintings. Each stroke of the brush is a note struck in a visual concerto; any mistake is as obvious to the viewer as hearing an orchestra member hit a wrong note.

It is fascinating and illuminating to visit artists in their studios. A chance to talk to a painter or sculptor about their work is always revealing. It can also be disconcerting when the artist in question suddenly jumps up without warning and makes a tiny alteration to his or her work. Such occurrences are not unusual. Artists are constantly thinking big picture, fine detail. None more so than Luc Tuymans.

The Belgian artist is not someone prone to artistic navel-gazing. It would undermine his work. The haunting atmosphere for which his paintings are admired is designed specifically with the viewer in mind. It is an approach that has made him one of the most revered and highly prized painters working today.

Tuymans lives and works in Antwerp, the city in which he was born and raised. His studio is located in a nondescript side street not far from the municipal masterpiece that is Antwerpen-Centraal railway station. Tuymans's place is not nearly as grand. It looks more like a tradesman's lock-up than an artist's studio. At least, it does from the outside. But step beyond the dull gray shutter and you enter another Wonderland.

A long airless passageway slopes upwards towards two large glass doors, behind which lies the studio. It is a massive, warehouse-like space. But that is not its most striking feature. The light is. An even blue-silver glow illuminates its white-walled open-plan rooms, an effect produced in part by its proximity to the North Sea, but accentuated by a fine translucent film that has been fitted to the rows of roof lights piercing the studio's ceiling.

The weather was miserable, gray and overcast when I visited, but when I looked up through those roof lights I could have been in the Mediterranean in June, so bold and blue did the sky appear.

> Me: *That's clever.*
> Luc: *The architect got it wrong. The light should not be like this.*
> Me: *What don't you like?*
> Luc: *It's too blue. And in the summer it casts shadows.*
> Me: *Oh. Still.*

The Belgian artist then lights the first of what would be many, many cigarettes.

Me: Don't you worry about that [smoking] killing you?
Luc: It won't.
Me: How do you know?
Luc: My mother smoked all her life. It did her no harm. It's
   genetic.
Me: Oh. Still.

The studio has paintings hanging on each of its six walls. Some are small, about one foot square. Others are much bigger, between one foot five and eleven feet in length. They are all on stretchers (Tuymans never frames his paintings) except one, which he finished the day before. It is a large canvas informally pinned to the wall, giving it the appearance of a loose-fitting shirt: edges curling, shallow contours billowing beneath it.

It depicts a diorama, a small-scale replica of a scene painted as an homage to Marcel Duchamp's controversial late work, *Étant Donnés* (1946–66). It is typical of Tuymans to take a pre-existing piece of visual art—it could be a photograph or a magazine clipping— as the basis for his own invention. It is too soon to judge the quality of this particular painting; it is in a raw state, but I still found it very telling. Not so much the picture itself, but what surrounded it.

A wide border of empty canvas framed his painting. Within these edgelands were sizeable splodges and dabs of paint, the normally unseen evidence that Tuymans uses this outer space as a mixing palette. Better than a hand-held board, he says, the canvas's rim being handier, more expansive and helpfully proximate to the image. This means when he steps back from the fine detail of actually painting in order to look at the big picture he is creating, he can check against the actual image to see if he has correctly mixed his paint before applying the next color.

And this is especially important to Tuymans. Not aesthetically, but practically. He works very quickly. All his paintings are started and finished in a single day.

> *Me: Do you ever come in the next morning and make changes?*
> *Luc: No.*
> *Me: Never?*
> *Luc: Not really.*
> *Me: Why?*
> *Luc: It's a habit.*
> *Me: But what if it's not finished?*
> *Luc: It's finished.*
> *Me: How do you know?*
> *Luc [lighting a cigarette]: I know.*

He paints using a technique known as wet-on-wet, where the paint never has time to dry. Corrections can be difficult—things can quickly get messy. Which makes him a particularly good artist to observe in the process of thinking big and small at the same time. Because the only way he can succeed in finishing a painting of such quality in a day is by having a detailed, preconceived grand plan.

The starting point for one of his paintings is not the moment he steps up, paintbrush charged, and addresses the naked canvas for the first time. Nor is it the night before, as he mulls the possibilities over dinner. It often begins months—sometimes years—before, when a random image has caught his eye. I don't know how long he had been contemplating the Duchamp homage, but I do know that the idea for the three portraits that hung on the first wall of his studio came to him six months earlier when he visited Edinburgh.

Tuymans had travelled to the Scottish capital in the summer, when its famous arts festivals were in full swing. While in the city he had gone to the university's Talbot Rice Gallery, where he had seen three portraits by the eighteenth-century Scottish portraitist Sir Henry Raeburn. They were of major figures from the Enlightenment: William Robertson, John Robison and John Playfair. Tuymans went to his pocket, reached for his iPhone and took photos of them.

Luc: Do you want to see?
Me: Sure.
Luc: What do you think?
Me: They're a bit blurry.
Luc: I love that! It's why I won't upgrade my phone.
Me: Because it takes lousy pictures?
Luc: Yes!

He is not being obtuse. For a man whose stock-in-trade is making paintings that appear to have a ghostly veil in front of them, it is useful to have a device that is able to suggest a similar effect. Tuymans does blurry. Raeburn did not.

Luc: I first saw one of his paintings in a gallery in Ghent.
Me: Oh?
Luc: He paints in a very straightforward way.
Me: What do you like about his work?
Luc: The dark palette. The simplicity.
Me: And the portraits?

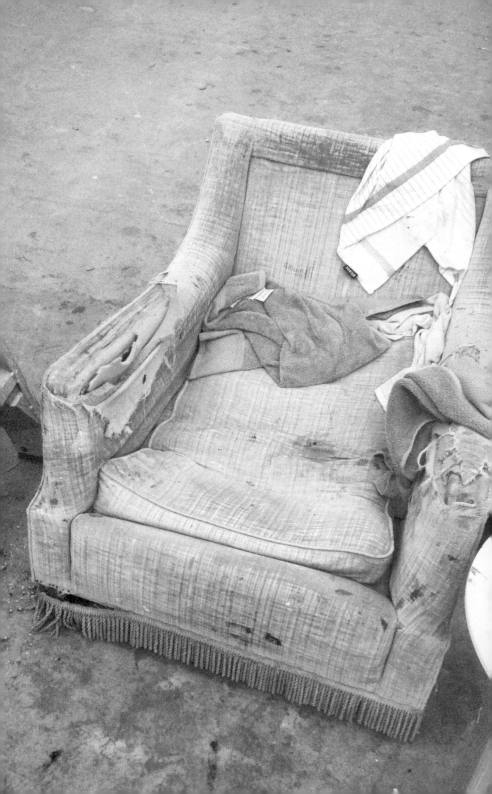

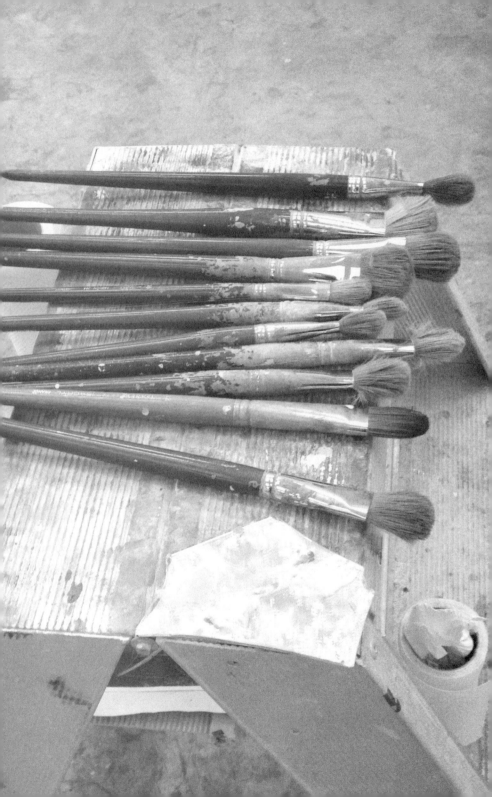

Luc: They are men of the Scottish Enlightenment.

Me: Yes.

Luc: Rational. Untouched by the British class system.

Me: I think they were all knighted.

Luc [walking towards his portraits]: You see the blue?

Each one of his three head portraits is made in response to Raeburn's originals, but with Tuymansesque modifications (see color section). The most obvious of which is his decision to aggressively crop and zoom into the faces of the three men, depicting only their noses, eyes and mouths. This wasn't a haphazard choice but a planned approach, inspired by the enlarged photocopies he made of the portraits on his return from Scotland. When he looked at them he noticed that the process of magnifying the images had caused the areas where the light caught the men's heads in the original paintings to turn from white to a cold light blue, most notably around their facial features.

The big picture of the past can bring in the fine detail of the present.

He liked it, and elected to use the blue as a painterly device to unite the series, hence his rationale for focusing in on the area where the blue-white transformation was at its most pronounced. In effect, Tuymans's paintings have been made from the fine detail of Raeburn's portraits. They are very striking. In fact, to my eyes, they are much more powerful than the originals. Tuymans has made these grand men of the eighteenth century appear vital and contemporary: the big picture of the past brought into the fine detail of the present.

And that's precisely the reaction the Belgian artist is hoping to elicit. He has used this group of three highly respectable thinkers as an enticement into the unknowable, unfathomable waters of Tuymans World. He wants to make us anxious. That is his starting point. Before he even contemplates producing any painting, there is the overriding framework into which he already knows it must fit: his style. That is the ultimate big picture he must keep in mind when painting the fine detail.

And a vital part of the Tuymans technique is to grab your attention when your guard is down by making paintings that initially appear more ephemeral than ethereal. When you first look at the three portraits they are underwhelming, almost childish in their simplicity. And then something catches your eye. You are not quite sure what, but something definitely has. You look again.

"Creativity is more than just being different. Making the simple, awesomely simple, that's creativity." Charles Mingus

And he's got you! Before you know it, you are staring into his hazy painting, looking beyond its foggy surface, searching for something concrete and clear. A story starts to build in your head about this vaguely recognizable character about whom you know nothing but who is mysterious enough for you to want to know more. The artist has used his imagination to fire yours.

He told me how he does it.

Luc: Every painting has a point of entry.
Me: What do you mean?
Luc: A small detail that catches your eye and draws you in.
Me: Preconceived by you?

Luc: Of course.

Me: Like what?

Luc: Sometimes it is invisible. The viewer cannot tell. It could be a very fine line, a tiny crack even.

Me: Can you show me on one of the portraits?

Luc: Sure. It's here [he jabs a finger towards the left eye]. At the top of the socket. It's much darker, more intense. That's the entry point. Believe me.

I do. It is a trick employed by many painters, from Jan van Eyck to Edward Hopper—both of whom are major influences on Tuymans. But perhaps the best exponent of this fine art was another northern European painter who was active back in the seventeenth century.

"Every painting has a point of entry. A small detail that catches your eye and draws you in."
Luc Tuymans

Johannes Vermeer was one of the great masters from the Dutch Golden Age. He lived in Delft, seventy-five miles along the coast from Tuymans's studio in Antwerp. Not much is known about him, other than that he had a wife and numerous children who were bankrupted due to his unpaid bills when he died.

Unlike Luc Tuymans, Vermeer worked very slowly and produced relatively few paintings. Those that have survived are exquisite in their rendering of light and form. They also benefit from the subtle touches he added, which coax you towards them with a "Drink Me" type of allure. You can find these almost imperceptible details in all his paintings, but the one that has pulled me in with the most irresistible force is

Girl with a Pearl Earring (1665) (see color section). Some of her magnetism is undoubtedly down to celebrity: a once ignored young lady is now world-famous thanks to Tracy Chevalier's best-selling book and the subsequent movie. But the reason she is so feted has more to do with the secrets she harbors about her creator's technique.

Up until 1994, they were shrouded underneath a ghastly yellow varnish that some well-meaning but misguided art restorer had applied in the 1960s. Fortunately conservation— as art restoration is now known—has come on a lot since the smoke-tinted days of the mid-twentieth century, when irreversible damage was done to many important paintings. Thankfully, though, not to Vermeer's masterpiece, which has now been returned to something approaching its original condition.

Vermeer's paintings are exquisite in their rendering of light and form. The subtle touches he added coax you towards them.

If there is anyone who has to constantly think about the big picture and small details it is the conservator charged with returning priceless paintings to their former glory. The job involves working inch by inch, taking samples, carrying out tests and generally treading as carefully as a mother checking on her sleeping baby. Any tiny intervention affects the entire canvas, physically and visually. There is no room for mistakes, which is why everything conservators do nowadays is reversible.

The team working on restoring *Girl with a Pearl Earring* had to remove the discolored ochre glaze before carefully taking off the patches of black paint that had been added long after the artist was dead. Finally, and after much painstaking work, they were left with an image far closer to the one painted by the Dutch master. The girl's late-twentieth-century facelift had brought back the vibrancy of the artist's bright palette, with his effervescent light reappearing from the gloom. But something wasn't quite right. There was a painted reflection on the bottom of the girl's earring that seemed a bit obvious, a bit gratuitous for Vermeer.

When the point of entry to the picture changes, it alters our reading of it.

The conservators X-rayed the image, studied the area with a magnifying glass, and eventually identified the problem. Vermeer, the most discriminating of artists, was not responsible for the heavy-handed effect on the earring: it was a flake of paint that had fallen from another part of the picture and been discolored by some wet filler applied during a previous restoration.

The technicians gingerly removed the offending fragment and then stood back to admire their work. And were surely amazed by what they saw. Not necessarily by their own handiwork but by what they could see now that the eye-catching flake had been removed. The point of entry to the picture had changed, which in turn altered the reading of it.

Luc Tuymans would have been amused. Vermeer's portrait is not altogether dissimilar to those produced by the Belgian. Both artists play with ambiguity and mystery, presenting us with fictional characters that seem real. Their subjects look back at us as if we know them, or they know us.

It is disconcerting. Tuymans's portraits are like visions from beyond the grave, while Vermeer's girl stares directly into our eyes, implying a relationship with us. Is it a look of innocence? She is very young. But then comes the moment when we see what those conservators saw for the first time in 1994.

In the corner of her mouth is an almost imperceptible dot of pink paint. It is the tiniest spot of pigment, but enough to draw your eyes to her lips, which are suggestively parted. Suddenly those innocent eyes look knowing, the pearl earring telling, the blue scarf alluring. What was at first a charming image becomes a charged portrait. And, in an instant, you are hers, and it only took a minuscule dab of pink paint to capture you.

Vermeer's tiny detail reveals the big picture.

This is the point of entry to Vermeer's magnificent painting: a tiny detail that reveals the big picture. It is strange to think that it had been lost to generations, forced as they were to come through another entry point—the highlight on her earring—which the artist had never intended.

I can't imagine such a thing happening with a Luc Tuymans painting while he is still alive. He is meticulous in every aspect of his work, both in how it is made and how it is shown. Nothing is left to chance.

Me: What's that?
Luc [unfolding a large piece of paper]: It's a plan.
Me: What of?
Luc: The layout for my next exhibition where I'll show these
    paintings [he gestures to the ten or so paintings hanging on
    his studio wall].

Me: You've already decided on the layout?
Luc: Sure.
Me: What about the curators?
Luc: I've shown them.
Me: Do you always plan your exhibitions?
Luc: Yes. It's the first thing I do.
Me: After you've finished painting, right?
Luc: No. Before I start.

Luc Tuymans plans an entire exhibition before his brush has even touched a canvas. How is that for thinking about the macro and the micro concurrently? Here is an artist who conceives every new set of paintings as an ensemble, like a composer writing a symphony. Each image is strategically placed to strike a specific note at a specific moment, and to catch the eye in a particular way. The colors he plans to use in one painting—such as the unifying blue in the portraits—are then echoed throughout the others. Themes are set, ideas explored.

At this stage he is an architect designing a building—it is a paper exercise. It is also one of the reasons he is able to work so fast when it comes to making the actual paintings. He has done most of the thinking beforehand, from choosing the colors of the walls on which his pictures will hang, to deciding on the scale of each image in relation to its physical location and proximity to his other work. Everything is fixed ahead of time.

And only then does Luc Tuymans get down to the business of painting. A canvas is pinned to the wall with a reference image placed to one side. There is a small table nearby on which unmixed oil paints have been squeezed out of tubes in chromatic order. Next to it is an aluminum foot-ladder on which eleven green-handled paintbrushes rest. Dotted about are some old rags, paint-thinning agents, a tape measure, a hammer and a couple of water bottles. There is a single beaten-up old armchair, the wooden frame of which is exposed in places where the cover has ripped and foam padding disintegrated.

He starts every painting by applying the lightest colors. This can take up to three hours. It is the stage of the process during which he can lose confidence; he finds it unsettling. This is the period when he is focusing solely on the fine detail and knows it is when he is most likely to get lost. Only when he begins to apply the darker tones to create the first elements of contrast, when a recognizable form starts to appear, does he begin to sense whether or not the painting will work out as he planned. Most do, some don't.

Luc Tuymans plans an entire exhibition before his brush has even touched a canvas. How is that for thinking about the macro and micro concurrently?

Throughout, he keeps a paint-splattered fragment of broken mirror nearby, which he occasionally reaches for to check on how the image appears from different angles.

Me: Why not step back and look?
Luc: It takes too much time.
Me: Oh.

He doesn't listen to the radio or music; he just stands and paints. He goes into a zone where he stops thinking and, he says, allows his "intelligence to go through my hand." The silence is an attempt, I suppose, to be at one with his paintings, which he describes as "mute," and "stunned." He says he prefers the effect rendered by cheaper paints, finds them more immediate. The whole thing is quite low-fi.

When the work is finished he goes home. If he doesn't like what he sees when he returns the next morning, he throws it out. If it passes muster he asks an assistant to put it on stretchers, when, he thinks, the image changes, "it becomes something else."

Much depends on the thought given to context and content before a pen or paintbrush is lifted.

Luc Tuymans is a specialist in the art of making, in understanding how the big picture and the fine detail must interact. Even the notion of conceiving an entire exhibition before he has painted a picture has a bigger thought behind it. A bigger thought that illustrates the minute levels of detail in which he deals.

The reason he plans his shows as a single coherent entity is not for entirely artistic reasons. It is a tactic to make sure his work continues to be shown in major museums long after he is gone. He realizes that nobody is going to buy all the paintings from one show, and that the group will inevitably be separated and scattered across the world. Some might well never be seen again, having been locked away in a museum's storage facility or behind an oligarch's security gates.

But, Tuymans speculates, if they are presented as a suite of interrelating pictures that only make real sense when hung together, there is bound to be an ambitious curator who some day feels compelled to reunite them for a special exhibition. The upshot of which would be to recall all the paintings from their various hiding places, returning them, and Tuymans, to the public eye.

In this regard Tuymans is like any other artist or individual involved in making and creating. So much depends on the thought given to context and content before a pen or paintbrush is lifted. Creativity is like a game of chess, where the best players are those who can think several moves ahead without losing sight of the immediate situation.

7. ARTISTS HAVE A
POINT OF VIEW

We know that no two people see things in exactly the same way. Ask ten people to describe the same view having seen it at the same time in the same conditions and you will have ten distinct descriptions. They won't necessarily be wildly different, but they'll be different enough to be identifiable as singular entities.

The same would apply if you and I went to see a film together. We would sit and watch the movie but we wouldn't come to identical conclusions about it. Our judgments would differ, based on our own unique filters, which are informed by our personal prejudices and mood.

"ONE EYE SEES, THE OTHER FEELS."

Paul Klee

It is an aspect of our makeup as humans that can drive sports fans into a frenzy, particularly when a referee perceives an in-game incident in a way that contradicts the fans' opinion. But when it comes to creativity this quirk of our nature is a gift to be prized. Our unique way of seeing leads to the choices we make, which differentiates our work from everybody else's. Our point of view is our signature.

Every decision we take in any creative process—whether we are decorating our bedroom or designing a dress—is based on our personal opinion: paint not wallpaper, strapless not halter-neck.

One of the more enjoyable aspects of creativity is the way it celebrates and rewards our oddness and idiosyncrasies. Individual peculiarities, which are often seen by society as a weakness, become a strength: a defining characteristic that gives us a unique filter on our view of the world and how the world views us.

Our point of view is our signature.

And, as we are all likely to end up being pigeonholed to some extent, we might as well take some control of the situation.

Alfred Hitchcock did. When you hear his name you don't think of family-friendly animated movies, or inter-galactic sci-fi epics; you associate it with tense noir thrillers. His point of view was to give us "a glimpse into the world that proves horror is nothing but reality." Hitchcock believed we needed and wanted frightening, and that he was the man to do it.

Let's be clear, a point of view is not the same as a style. It is what you say, not the way you say it. And in the creativity game you are not really a player unless you have something to say. It is a principle the French romantic painter Eugène

Delacroix eloquently summed up when he said: "What makes men of genius, or rather what inspires their work, are not new ideas; instead they are pressed by the idea that what has been said has not been said enough."

The German Expressionists who emerged traumatized in mind and body after World War One exemplified Delacroix's definition of genius. Otto Dix was a naive young painter when the war began; he thought it was a good thing at first and enthusiastically volunteered to be a machine-gunner. He was sent to the Western Front in 1915, and later to the Somme at the height of the Allied offensive.

In the creativity game you are not a player unless you have something to say.

He survived, but he was scarred both mentally and physically for life. He marked the tenth anniversary of the war's outbreak by producing a devastating cycle of prints called *Der Krieg*, or *The War* (1924). They are an unflinching account, and condemnation, of what he saw and participated in. Death, decay and contorted bodies abound in images that are made even more unsettling by Dix choosing the technique of etching, in which acid burns into the printing plate.

He had taken Francisco Goya's equally horrific print series *The Disasters of War* (1810–20) as a template. The Spanish artist had produced this during his country's long-running conflict with Napoleon's French Empire a century earlier. Dix clearly felt that what Goya had said about war had not been said enough.

The message may have been the same but the messenger was not. Both artists had witnessed the ghastly barbarism of violent conflict, but saw it in slightly different ways. Goya is more graphic in his visual descriptions of acts of extreme violence, whereas Dix focuses his attention on its aftermath and immediate consequences.

This variance illustrates Delacroix's point about genius and, by extension, creativity. He is saying that it is not the core idea—or subject—that is important, but what an individual is inspired to say about it that is new or different. And that is where many of us come unstuck.

Having something original to express is one of the biggest obstacles to overcome in the creative process. We have heard of writer's block, but the same loss of inspiration also happens to artists, inventors and scientists. So it's hardly surprising that those of us who do not earn our living by creating day-in day-out can often draw a similar blank.

The message may have been the same but the messenger was not.

Getting stuck is a frustration every artist of every type has to face at one time or another. But fortunately for them and for us there are ways to overcome such blocks.

One method that has been proven to work time and again is to move. A change of scene literally changes your point of view: the disruption activates your senses, which are stimulated by the unfamiliar; you see and experience life differently. An impulse to capture and express your feelings is heightened, which is why we like to take photographs when away from home.

You discover subjects that were previously obscured, and perceive afresh those with which you were already familiar.

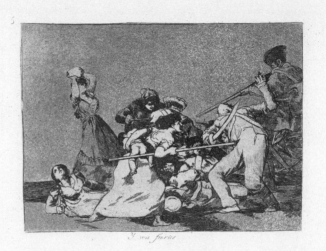

Otto Dix, from *Der Krieg*, 1924

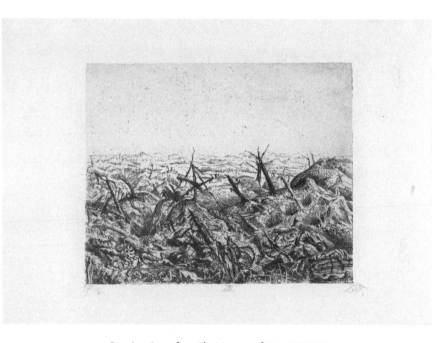

Francisco Goya, from *The Disasters of War*, 1810–20

The move might entail changing jobs, or home, or city. Or, in the case of the celebrated contemporary artist Peter Doig, changing continent.

Doig makes eerie, sparsely populated paintings that are typically—although not exclusively—set in landscapes in which one or two figures loom. His characters have a habit of looking lost or bemused—which I suspect is how the artist himself has felt from time to time.

Peter Doig had a peripatetic childhood. He was born in Scotland, which was followed by some early years in Trinidad, and then his parents took him off to Canada, where he grew up. He came to London and went to art school in the late 1970s, returned to Canada to live in Montreal, and then came back to London in 1989 for more studying. It was this itinerant upbringing that gave him the impulse to explore the unknowable quality of landscapes in his art. But he had a problem: he didn't know what he wanted to say about them.

In that respect he was different from most artists who move for inspiration. For the majority it is a case of a new location providing some much-needed new source material. The most obvious example of this is probably Paul Gauguin and his late nineteenth-century Tahitian odyssey. The French Post-Impressionist's response to his new environment was typical of an artist in search of a muse. He gratefully discovered an exciting, exotic subject and quickly produced the colorful, stylized images that have gone on to influence many artists, including Peter Doig.

But while Doig admired Gauguin's paintings, he did not enjoy the same artistic epiphany and productivity in response to a new location. On the contrary, he felt creatively even more lost. So, while he was happy living in London among other aspiring artists, he was frustrated that he couldn't find anything original or interesting to say about the city. Until he found himself at the Canadian Embassy in central London, where he leafed through some of the tourist brochures laid out in the reception area. They featured the normal set of clichéd images of idealized Canadian vistas and sublime scenery. He put them down. And then . . . eureka!

Doig realized what had been holding him back. It wasn't moving to a new environment that inspired him, it was moving from an old one. Or, as he put it to me, "I have to leave somewhere before I can paint it." He had discovered his point of view.

He went back to his London studio and started to paint. *Hitch Hiker* (1989–90) was one of the first images to emerge. It depicts a red truck in the middle distance traveling out West. Its lights are on, the sky suggests an impending storm, and the landscape is open and vast. And empty, barring a few distant trees. The eponymous *Hitch Hiker* is nowhere to be seen.

**"I have to leave somewhere before I can paint it."
Peter Doig**

Peter Doig, the Artist, had arrived. He now had what he says all artists need, which is "something to run with." His "something" was rather more complex than painting atmospheric Canadian landscapes. On reflection, what he really wanted to say wasn't specifically about anywhere: Canada was simply fulfilling the role of messenger. The message was about memories. Not sentimental recollections, but the very notion of memories: what they are, the part they play, and the habit they have of evolving into a collage of experiences.

The landscape he was actually exploring was metaphysical, the ethereal space that separates the real and the remembered. Call it the uncanny, or surreal, or strange: Doig's paintings take us to a place that has the appearance of reality but is in fact an illusion, one that only exists in our mind's eye—like memories.

Doig said he "went from feeling I didn't have ideas, to feeling like I had a lot of ideas. I got this inspiration I could never possibly have imagined."

Once we discover what we want to say, everyday life can become a potential source of creative stimulation.

Once the creative block is lifted and we discover what we want to say and express, a lot of what we took for granted—the mundane aspects of everyday life—becomes potential sources of creative stimulation. It is a truism that Nora Ephron—the American journalist, essayist and screenwriter—had passed down to her by her mother, who said, "Everything is copy."

Even skiing. Why the majority of artists have chosen to ignore such an internationally popular pastime as skiing for over a century is anyone's guess. Too bourgeois, maybe? If so, that's just the sort of dogma Doig likes to counter and question. Plus, as with any neglected theme, it gave him a clear run at the subject.

Ski Jacket (1994) (see color section) features many more human figures than is usual for his paintings. This is an image crowded with people skiing, although none of them are recognizable as such. Individuals are represented by a mass of tiny colored dots with microscopic splinters for legs. The centerpiece of the picture is a dark and dense copse of pine trees, which draws you in with all the irresistible negative energy of a black hole. From this darkness radiates an incandescent blast of whites, pinks and yellows. Doig is alluding to the extreme form of seeing we experience when out skiing: a kind of psychedelic trip fuelled by the bright light, Day-Glo skiwear and filtered goggles.

But I suspect the painting is not really about skiing at all. Rather, it is about being Peter Doig, about being human. The painting is a visual contemplation of a universally uncomfortable sensation we all know too well: the feeling of awkwardness. Those dotty figures are first-time skiers struggling down a mountain in Japan: exhilarated but embarrassed.

It is a retrospective, semi-fictional painting designed to disorient, and perhaps to convey and reflect upon the unsettling nature of moving. Transience, memory and atmosphere seem to be Doig's subjects. In 2002 he left London for Trinidad, one of his childhood staging posts. And there he remains, for now. Maybe he'll move again if and when he gets stuck.

Of course, you don't have to live the life of a nomad to find a subject to inspire you. Nor do you have to change continent on a regular basis to engender a feeling of nostalgia and disorientation. As Rembrandt van Rijn discovered.

I know it seems unlikely for such a prestigious, prodigious artist, but the Dutch master is said to have also suffered from a creative block. According to scholars, it happened in 1642 when he was at the height of his success. The artist was happily married, professionally respected, and settled in a splendid house he had recently bought in Amsterdam. Life was good. He was the go-to portraitist for the rich and influential, among whom was a local civic guard company who had recently commissioned him to paint a group portrait, which would eventually come to be known as *The Night Watch* (1642). What could possibly go wrong?

A lot, as it turned out. Starting with the death of his beloved wife, Saskia. She was Rembrandt's great love, and with her passing came an intractable gloom that descended over the painter. His mood wasn't improved by a few snide comments made by some of the sitters in *The Night Watch*, who grumbled that their features were poorly painted. This insult was compounded by a small group of younger painters in Amsterdam who had copied Rembrandt's style and were now taking his clients.

It is the artist's job to pay attention to prompts, to trust their feelings and instincts.

The money started to dry up, a situation made worse when the nurse employed to look after his young son sued him for not marrying her. To add to his woes, his masterpiece, *The Night Watch*, turned out to be the culmination of a theatrical, all-action style of painting he had spent the past twenty years exploring, leaving him devoid of ideas. He was thirty-six years old, miserable, lonely, and had nothing left to say. Rembrandt was having a mid-life crisis.

He had lost his way; he no longer had a point of view. The flamboyance that had marked his life and art was gone. He retreated into an increasingly introspective state. But in his anguish lay the solution to his creative impasse. He found that the deeper he descended into his miserable state, the more acutely he felt his emotions. The copyists made him angry, high society irritated him, and the memory of Saskia haunted him.

Rembrandt recognized that inspiration comes in many guises, and it is the artist's job to pay attention to prompts, to trust their feelings and instincts. He did. And discovered a new subject about which he had a very clear point of view: the melancholic nature of aging.

He responded to this new stimulus by adapting his style. The refined brushstrokes that had served him so well were put aside in favour of a more expressive technique. The new, forlorn Rembrandt would load his brush and apply the thick oil paint to his canvas in broad sweeps and emphatic dabs. The change gave his pictures an extra dimension and weight, both symbolically and literally. It also marked his work out from anybody else's—this was a signature style that came from a torment within, something that could not be easily plagiarized.

Rembrandt discovered a new subject about which he had a very clear point of view: the melancholic nature of aging.

Rembrandt had navigated his way out of an artistic dead-end in a manner he could not have imagined a year or two earlier. The vulnerability of the human soul was a theme he would explore for the rest of his life, in religious scenes, etchings and commissions. But it is the fifteen self-portraits he painted in the last two decades of his life that communicate

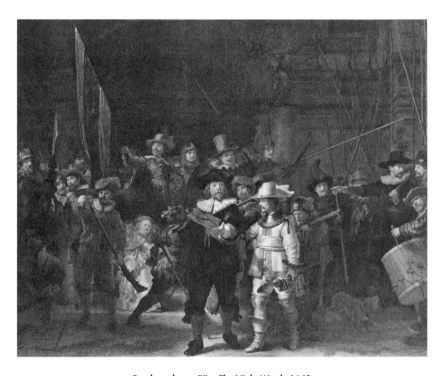

Rembrandt van Rijn, *The Night Watch*, 1642

most consistently and powerfully the inner sadness and outward dignity that came with his advancing years.

None is more poignant than *Self Portrait at the Age of 63* (1669) (see color section). Here we see Rembrandt as he saw himself a few months before he died. His face is one of defiant resignation. His mid-life losses have been compounded by bankruptcy, the death of his lover, and most heartbreakingly that of his son Titus. But below his gray curly hair, his rheumy eyes and his bulbous nose is a faint twitch at the outer edges of his mouth, suggesting a tentative smile. Is this the artist putting a brave face on things, or showing us that in this final chapter of his life there has been some good news at last, in the shape of a longed-for granddaughter?

> **"We have to continually be jumping off cliffs and developing our wings on the way down."**
> **Kurt Vonnegut**

Rembrandt worked to the very end of his life without ever taking a step back. With his last self-portrait we see an artist still willing to innovate, to take risks, to submit himself to honest self-examination and to be frank about what he finds. He turned introspection into an art form, and the self-portrait into a moving and philosophical expression of humanity.

None of this would have happened if Rembrandt had made paintings that were impartial or impersonal. Opinion is what drove him forward, and it will be opinion that compels any of us to make something exceptional and different. If we want our ideas to be seen and heard it is essential we have a point of view and something to say.

But what about those people who are not seen or heard, either in person or through representation? Are they invisible? Yes, they are, according to the American artist Kerry James Marshall. That is his point of view.

Marshall is a black man who found himself in a white man's world when he entered the realm of Western art. It was an environment in which he didn't merely feel out of place, but totally non-existent. When he went around art museums and galleries as a young student at the Otis Art Institute in Los Angeles he encountered an overwhelming sense of absence. He discovered that there were almost no black subjects depicted in the entire history of Western art, nor could he find any black artists who had been included in the story.

Before he made these visits Marshall was struggling to find a subject he wanted to paint. He wasn't sure what—if anything—he had to communicate. He now knew. Peter Doig found inspiration in physical spaces, Rembrandt in personal places: Marshall's was in the politics of race.

Peter Doig found inspiration in physical spaces, Rembrandt in personal places, Marshall in the politics of race.

As soon as he graduated he found a studio and got to work. The idea was simple, to insert black people into the Western canon. He had spent his life being told to appreciate paintings by white artists of white people; he reckoned it wasn't unreasonable to expect some reciprocation.

He knew it wouldn't be easy. He had witnessed first-hand the marginalization of black people from white culture, having grown up in the American South in the late 1950s and early 1960s. His parents subsequently moved the family to LA in 1963, settling in the same neighborhood in which the infamous Watts riots would take place a couple of years later.

The arts in general have been slow to incorporate and acknowledge non-white, non-Western voices. It has taken Hollywood half a century to make a biopic about Martin Luther King Jr., which it eventually did with *Selma* (2014). The British actor David Oyelowo, who played Dr. King in the movie, told me that in his opinion the game is "rigged."

This is what Marshall was—and still is—up against in his quest for black representation in Western art. Nevertheless, he is playing the game, and with some success. The prestigious LACMA museum in LA was the first major institution to buy one of his paintings: a

"We're not robots. Life is more exciting when you have an opinion."
Cheryl Lynn Bruce

large group portrait called *De Style* (1993, see color section). The title is a reference to Piet Mondrian's early twentieth-century abstract art movement, but there is nothing abstract about Marshall's picture.

It is set in an African-American barbershop populated by four customers and a barber, all of whom are black. Iconography from popular African-American culture abounds. Horizontal and vertical lines allude to Mondrian's modernist aesthetic, as does the painting's palette, which largely consists of the Dutchman's beloved primary colors.

You might think, then, that Marshall was aiming to place his painting in the Western modernist canon. And he is, partly. But his ultimate objective is to align his art to the great works produced by the great masters. Yes, by painting *De Style* he has forced his art into the story of European modernism, which is dominated by white, Western males.

But the painting to which it strikes me as being a contemporary companion piece is *The Night Watch*. The allusions to it are formal and subtle. For instance, Rembrandt paints his white figures emerging out of a black background with a light foreground. Marshall reverses the composition for emphasis by having his black figures appearing out of a white background with a black foreground.

The painting is an example of the American artist's wit and intelligence, which has seen him become a prominent figure in the art world. When I visited his studio in Chicago it was full of impressive paintings responding to other past masters, from Manet to Velázquez, all of which were set in modern America and featured only black people. Six months later, they were hanging in the pristine Mayfair gallery of his London art dealer. They were all sold for significant sums, some, I believe, to those same museums he once visited and where he saw nothing of the world he recognized.

Marshall has made some very good art by having a specific, personal point of view. It is a distinctiveness that runs right through his life, as I found out when I mistakenly knocked on the door of his house before eventually finding his studio a few blocks down the road.

His wife, the actress Cheryl Lynn Bruce, answered the door. She could not disguise her irritation when I showed up at the Marshall home instead of the artist's studio as planned. She quizzed me, checked my credentials and after a while kindly invited me in.

Did I want a slice of her freshly made cake?

I did.

She pointed up to a shelf of plates stacked vertically in a rack above the sink. "Choose one," she said. I must have looked nonplussed. "Choose a plate," she repeated. And then explained that she collects plates, but only ever one of any type. It was up to the guest to decide which one would be theirs for the duration of the stay. "We're not robots," she said. "Life is more exciting when you have an opinion."

"TO CREATE ONE'S WORLD IN ANY OF THE ARTS TAKES COURAGE."

Georgia O'Keeffe

8. ARTISTS ARE BRAVE

Courage is a quality we tend to associate with conflict. We honor soldiers for being courageous, and treat sports stars as heroes when they take on a superior opponent and win. David is a legend for overcoming Goliath.

It is in extreme circumstances that these courageous people show their mettle. They will go that little bit further, take the chance most of us wouldn't, and expose themselves to dangers others would avoid. I suppose the ultimate form of this type of courage is the heroism of those who risk their own lives to save others.

But there is another sort of courage . . .

There is a form of courage, a courage that's based on the same principle—personal vulnerability—but does not put the protagonist in any immediate physical danger. It is the psychological courage needed to stand up—unbidden—and express your feelings and ideas in public to a potentially hostile audience.

Of this type of bravery the legendary fashion designer Coco Chanel declared, "The most courageous act is still to think for yourself. Aloud."

This is what artists do, even though it leaves them exposed. They are, in a way, naked in front of the world, saying, "Look at me!" And they do this when they are not entirely sure what they have produced is any good. Creativity, as Henri Matisse said, "takes courage."

Psychological courage is needed to stand up and express your feelings and ideas in public.

Nobody wants to make a fool of themselves in public, to risk humiliation in front of friends, family or strangers. We are programmed not to put ourselves in such a position. We are born with an inclination towards self-doubt, particularly when it comes to creativity. Doubt is there to stop us at those moments when we feel confident—or foolish—enough to put the fruits of our creativity in the line of critical fire. It is at this moment that our modesty kicks in and stops us before we shame ourselves.

At the time it feels like a relief. It even feels quite good. Humility, after all, is an honorable quality. But not always when it comes to creativity, when it can be nothing more than a big sofa to hide behind. Daunting and unnatural as it

"THE MOST COURAGEOUS ACT IS STILL TO THINK FOR YOURSELF. ALOUD."

Coco Chanel

may seem, boldness is required to release ideas into the world, even though it can feel alien and arrogant. I mean, who do I think I am? Some kind of genius? Surely there are far more talented people than me out there who deserve the attention?

And so it goes: humility applies the handbrake to our creativity. In truth, we have chickened out. We wanted to share our ideas and originality with the world but we didn't dare. This is the sort of behavior Aristotle could have been referring to when he said, "You will never do anything in this world without courage."

The fact is, in order to create you have to take a leap of faith; not just in yourself, but also in your fellow man. You have to trust the world to judge you fairly. Yes, you will receive criticism. And yes, it will hurt. Sometimes a lot. You may well hear a chorus of disapproval.

But this sense of rejection will likely be no more than anybody else has endured; consider it a rite of passage. We all know the stories about the Beatles being turned down and how numerous publishers rebuffed J. K. Rowling. Did it stop them? No. Did it add to their resolve? Of course. As Virgil encouraged, "Blessings on your courage, boy; that's the way to the stars."

It certainly was for a thirty-two-year-old Italian artist called Michelangelo Buonarroti. He may well have had Virgil's words of fortitude ringing in his ears as he stood unsteadily atop some wooden scaffolding in the middle of Rome, the same city in which the ancient poet had spoken his wise words over a millennium earlier.

It was 1508, and the brilliant but tempestuous Michelangelo was not happy. His omnipotent patron Pope Julius II had recently cancelled a lucrative commission for him to sculpt the papal tomb. The artist was furious and had stormed out of Rome and gone back home to Florence.

A combination of Pope Julius's bullying and flattery got him to return, only for the artist to discover that a spiteful atmosphere had developed within the papal court. Michelangelo was suspicious—with good reason—that Donato Bramante, the Pope's favoured architect, was attempting to get him fired in favour of a young upstart known to all as Raphael, who had recently arrived on the scene.

Michelangelo had hoped his return would see the tomb commission reinstated, which, for him, was a dream job. Even for a sculptor as skilled and quick as he was, the task would have taken him at least twenty years to complete. And that, for a man in his early thirties at the beginning of the sixteenth century, was tantamount to a job for life. But it was not to be. The Pope had another assignment in

"The soul should always stand ajar, ready to welcome the ecstatic experience." Emily Dickinson

mind for him, which raised Michelangelo's paranoia about Bramante's and Raphael's scheming to fever pitch.

Julius II's uncle, Sixtus IV, had built a splendid new chapel when he was Pope a few decades earlier. It was a fine building that was duly named after the nepotistic pontiff. But by the time Julius rose to power his uncle's Sistine Chapel had already started to deteriorate to such an extent that major repairs to its fabric were required. One area that was particularly badly affected was the vast vaulted ceiling, which hangs sixty-eight feet above the chapel floor.

The Pope had many faults, but a lack of taste was not one of them. Julius was an aesthete and enthusiastic champion of the arts, and was determined that this most important and sacred building would have a painted ceiling to match. He instructed that it should be frescoed with twelve large figures of the Apostles, and Michelangelo was the man for the task.

But when the imperious Julius broke the news to the fiery Florentine—who was not known to be short of confidence himself—he got a reaction he neither wanted nor expected.

To take on the Sistine Chapel would mean risking everything for a commission he neither wanted nor felt equipped to undertake.

Michelangelo looked into the eyes of the one man in Rome you should not refuse and said no. He would not paint the ceiling of the Sistine Chapel, or the nave or its walls. He was a sculptor, not a painter. And he was definitely not a fresco painter, a speciality he had chosen not to develop after being taught the technique in a rudimentary fashion during his apprenticeship.

The Pope suspected Michelangelo was being petulant because he had withdrawn the tomb commission. And that probably had something to do with it. But the main reason Michelangelo reacted so angrily was because he genuinely didn't think he was capable of doing the job. He didn't consider himself a painter. What's more, he suspected Bramante and Raphael had persuaded the Pope to give him the responsibility knowing all too well that frescoing was beyond him. They were, to Michelangelo's mind, setting him up to fail.

It seems hardly credible, given what we now know, but

Michelangelo was in a similar position to the one the rest of us find ourselves in when taking on a new creative pursuit. He was frightened. He had so much to lose: his status as the finest artist in the land, his livelihood, and, worst of all, his self-confidence. To take on the Sistine Chapel would mean risking everything for a commission he neither wanted nor felt equipped to undertake.

And yet, eventually, he accepted.

You could argue that he came to realize he had no choice, but then his reputation was such that he already had a full order book of commissions waiting to be undertaken once he had finished working for the Pope. After all, this was the man who had recently given the world *David*, his sculptural masterpiece. He could have made his excuses, but he didn't. He took on a challenge every bit as great as the one his petrified David accepted from Goliath. His decision wasn't forced; it was an act of courage.

At first he tried to mitigate the risk by hiring reputable local painters. But they were either too slow or not up to his standards. He was on his own, right down to designing the scaffolding. And once that was in place and he was able to get up close to the ceiling, he saw the true extent of the technical and artistic problems that faced him. At which point he tried handing in his resignation once again.

He went back to the Pope and said it was hopeless; he couldn't do it. Fresco painting such a huge space, with wet paint and plaster dripping into his eyes, ears and mouth, and then drying before the composition was completed, was too difficult a task. Added to which, there were the problematic architectural idiosyncrasies of the Chapel's ceiling, and the inadequacies of the design that Pope Julius himself had specified for the space.

Julius listened to all of Michelangelo's concerns and complaints, and countered them one by one. Including the issue of what the overall visual scheme should look like, to which he bluntly told the artist to paint "what he liked."

Perhaps resigned to the fact that the Chapel would be the scene of his public humiliation, Michelangelo appears to have decided that if the commission was going to be seen as a failure, he might as well fail spectacularly. To which end he devised a design for the ceiling so complex and technically difficult that nobody could question his ambition even if they ridiculed the end result. He would portray in paint the story of the Bible from a papal point of view, with the major events running along the spine of the ceiling. This would consist of nine scenes from the Book of Genesis, starting with God separating light and darkness, and ending with a drunk and disgraced Noah. Its centerpiece would focus on the Creation of Adam and Eve.

Michelangelo decided that if the commission was going to be seen as a failure, he might as well fail spectacularly.

For the next four years Michelangelo painted day and night, barely sleeping, hardly ever drinking, and by all accounts not bothering to wash much either. He spent this time standing on his wooden scaffold, his face flat to the ceiling, head bent back, arms held aloft. The physical discomfort and mental exhaustion would have been the end of most of us.

But not Michelangelo. In October 1512, now in his late thirties, he completed his marathon task. He dismantled the scaffolding, had a bath, took a drink, and invited the Pope and his court to come and see what he—the amateur fresco painter—had achieved.

It must have been an astonishing moment for all present: for Michelangelo to see the reaction of the Pope's retinue, and for them to see his work. Given that the colors, compositions, ambition and scale of the work continue to leave visitors overawed today, we can only imagine that the papal party stood there with mouths and eyes wide open in amazement. Nothing like this had been produced before, or has been since. The sheer virtuosity of Michelangelo's painting, together with his exemplary technique, complete understanding of perspective and vivid imagination, is dazzling and unmatched.

Creativity does not exist in isolation. There would be no Sistine Chapel ceiling if it hadn't been for the dogged persistence of Pope Julius II.

The artist had faced down his enemies, his own technical shortcomings, his lack of confidence, and taken an enormous risk, for which we are all grateful. To return to Virgil, the world blessed Michelangelo's courage and his way to the stars.

But we should not forget this is a story that has another hero, another fearless protagonist. Creativity does not exist in isolation. It needs a nurturing environment in which it can flourish. And quite often that means having a patron or a supporter who will protect, enable, cajole and commission. There would be no Sistine Chapel ceiling for us all to enjoy if it hadn't been for the dogged persistence of Pope Julius II and his unwavering faith in Michelangelo's talent.

While Michelangelo worried about sinister plots against him being hatched by Bramante and Raphael, the Pope was happy to trust his own judgment. He believed Michelangelo was the only man to take on the Sistine Chapel, even though he knew Bramante doubted him. The Pope may have been an arrogant megalomaniac—not unlike his willful employee—but he was also a visionary, whose foresight and courage in backing his man gave the world one of its most enduring masterpieces.

Michelangelo is an example to us all. Any one of us hoping to explore new ideas must be daring. Society puts enormous pressure on us to conform. It functions when we all adhere to agreed systems. We obediently drive our cars on a designated side of the road, use money as the accepted mode of exchange for goods or services received, and patiently stand in queues. It works. If we didn't respect these social conventions chaos would ensue and society would collapse. But there is a hitch.

The status quo is not fixed. Like the planet on which we live, change is the only constant. People move, power shifts, and so opportunities arise. Societies evolve. The more aware among us, or those with specialist knowledge, can sense these adjustments and opportunities and respond accordingly. Scientists make discoveries based on a small piece of new information made available in an unrelated field. Entrepreneurs quickly identify new business openings. And artists modify their modes of expression to reflect a new age.

All three groups are fuelled by their imaginations; all rely on their creativity to inform their actions. And all three will face challenges realizing their ideas: society is very cautious when it comes to new concepts, which we tend to dismiss at first. It may seem counter-intuitive that artists, of all people, have to fight against the prevailing dogma and conservative attitudes. But the reality is they are operating in a commercial market in which art dealers want to present work they already know they can sell, collectors want to buy art their circle will recognize, and the establishment only wants what it knows and understands.

To break the rules and defy all these powerful parties takes enormous courage. Only a very bold artist would take them on, and even then they often need help. It generally requires (at least) two to take on the aesthetic status quo: an artist and a patron. The patron might be in the form of an art dealer, as was the case with the Impressionists, who had Paul Durand-Ruel to thank for supporting and selling their work and making them famous. Or it could be a wealthy collector like Peggy Guggenheim, who almost single-handedly launched Jackson Pollock's career, and in doing so paved the way for Abstract Expressionism.

There is, though, one way for an artist to present a radical new idea to the public without recourse to a patron. And that is by opting out of the system altogether. It takes a lot of courage. But if you are innovative, and brave, it can be done—as Banksy has ably demonstrated.

His politically charged cartoons were once described as the work of a "prankster" but have more recently been upgraded by museum curators, who speak of them in terms of being bona-fide artworks.

Banksy is now being appropriated by the very establishment system that he has been rebelling against for years. He has mocked it from the outside with his graffiti (now given the stamp of approval by curators, who call it Street Art), and from the inside with amusing interventions. Take the time he hung a small, worthless lump of rock among the exhibits on display at the venerated British Museum. He placed his piece of rubble—on which he had drawn (in marker pen) a caveman-like figure pushing a shopping trolley—in a gallery displaying carvings from classical antiquity. Accompanying it was a caption (typeset to fit into the museum's corporate style) which read:

> *This finely preserved example of primitive art dates from the Post-Catatonic era … most art of this type has unfortunately not survived. The majority is destroyed by zealous municipal officials who fail to recognize the artistic merit and historical value of daubing on walls.*

It remained alongside the ancient Egyptian and Greek antiquities for several days, until the museum either noticed or was alerted to its presence. It was typical of Banksy's provocative style: an uncomfortable truth wrapped in a cheeky joke.

In this case the joke was the rock; the uncomfortable truth was the "zealous municipal officials." Nobody wants to be cast as a jobsworth or a killjoy who tries to prevent ideas and ingenuity, but the fact is most of us are—or at least we're happy to sit back while others act on our behalf. The stories in art—and in culture more broadly—where high-ranking intellectual aesthetes have been responsible for attempting to quash creativity are legion, going all the way back to Plato and his anti-art *Republic*.

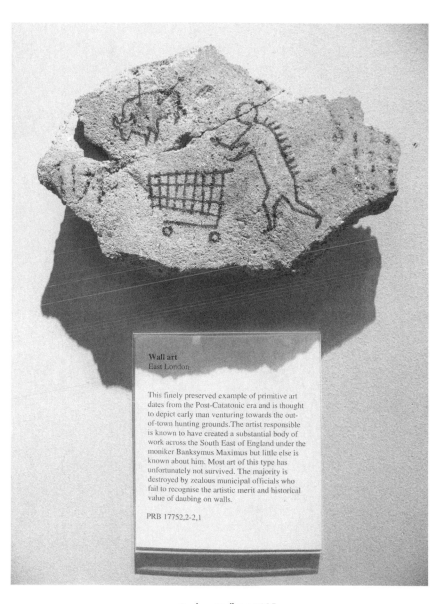

Banksy, *Wall Art,* **2005**

George Bernard Shaw described this latent philistinism when making notes to his play *Caesar and Cleopatra* (1898), in which he said of Julius Caesar: "He's a man of great common sense and good taste, meaning thereby a man without originality or moral courage."

We, the public and our official representatives, are not usually being stubbornly conservative or purposely small-minded. It's just that we are often unprepared for a new idea when it is first presented to us by an artist. He or she will have spent months—if not years—of inquiry, experiment and development in reaching a coherent creation, which we are then expected to understand and assimilate in moments. It is no surprise that we fail to do so. But the mistake we make—as George Bernard Shaw was pointing out—is that instead of trusting the artist, our natural inclination is to distrust and dismiss, threatened as we are by an unknown and potentially dangerous novelty we can't comprehend.

"Have no fear of perfection, you'll never reach it."
Salvador Dalí

It is on this hostile, stony ground of suspicion and suppression that creativity must try to flourish. It's a struggle. At best it's frustrating; at times it's dangerous. At worst, it's deadly. Which is why artists and creators of all types really do need to be brave.

Throughout the ages and right up to the present day, writers, directors, poets, composers and artists have been subjected to persecution, incarceration and even torture, for doing nothing more than expressing themselves though art. There is censorship in every country in the world. Sometimes it is the brutal and blatant suppression enforced by a dictatorial regime; at other times it is the more subtle insidiousness of politically correct dogma, bullying by single-issue groups, and corporate spin.

Recently, in the United Kingdom, I have seen theater productions canceled, comedians silenced, and images removed from a major museum website. In all cases the artist or artists didn't make the decision: they were, in effect, being censored. Meanwhile, in Beijing, the internationally renowned Chinese artist Ai Weiwei continues to be held under house arrest. From the solitude of his home he is taking on a mighty empire. Not with an army, or through terrorism, or within a political party—but with art.

There is this notion that art in all its shapes and forms is soft: a sideshow designed to entertain and amuse, and not really a serious matter. Ai Weiwei, Pussy Riot and countless others who have been, and still are, subjected to suppression suggest otherwise. Creativity is a powerful tool, which is why it has been feared by figures of authority from Plato to Putin. It is how we express ourselves. It gives a voice to democracy, and shape to a civilization. It is a platform for ideas and an agent of change. We should treat it with respect, and as both creators and citizens always try to be open-minded and generous-spirited.

Creativity gives a voice to democracy, and shape to a civilization.

It is, after all, our imagination that makes us human. Vincent van Gogh asked, "What would life be if we had no courage to attempt anything?" To which the answer is, I would have thought, boring, bordering on pointless.

9. ARTISTS PAUSE
FOR THOUGHT

If you visit any artist's studio there is one object you are pretty much guaranteed to see. It might be in the middle of the room, or tucked away to one side, next to a ladder or surrounded by jars of turpentine. It might even be covered by a dustsheet. Whatever the particular circumstances, it will be there: the artist's much loved but often battered old chair.

Its purpose is far greater than simply providing a weary painter or sculptor with a comfortable place to sit, although that is undoubtedly part of its function. It has a higher calling, which is to play a vital role in the creative process. The artist's chair is transformative.

WHEN ARTISTS SIT DOWN IN THEIR CHAIRS THEY STOP BEING THE CREATOR AND TURN INTO A CRITIC.

When artists sit down in their chairs they switch personas. They stop being the creator and turn into a critic. With the temperament of the most fastidious connoisseur, they look at what they have just created and evaluate their efforts. Their hyper-critical eyes scrutinize the work for insincerity, sloppiness and technical mistakes.

Sometimes, having identified a problem, they will jump up and make a small correction. Painters like David Hockney are known to do this almost as a matter of routine. He will finish painting, sit down and look at what he has done. His eyes will trace the surface of the canvas as if he were tracking the flight of a fly, darting to and fro, scanning the painting for problems. Sometimes they will see nothing untoward and he will lean back and light a cigarette. On other occasions they settle on one tiny area and narrow. This is when the revered British artist will rise out of his chair, grab a brush, charge it, and apply a dab of paint to the offending section.

Amazingly, it makes a real difference. He showed me where he had added a small dot of yellow paint to his massive painting *The Arrival of Spring in Woldgate, East Yorkshire* (2011). In a picture that is over thirty feet long and more than eleven feet tall, you would have thought the addition of a yellow petal no bigger than a small coin would be wholly incidental. But it wasn't. It subtly, but emphatically, altered the balance of the composition and the way it is read.

The most famous example of this type of post-hoc painterly intervention has to be the occasion when the English Romantic artist J. M. W. Turner found that his elegant seascape *Helvoetsluys* had been hung alongside John Constable's dramatic *Opening of Waterloo Bridge*. It happened at the annual Royal Academy exhibition in May 1832, the year's most prestigious art event. The two men were great rivals and highly competitive; they were not friends.

Constable's picture had taken him over ten years to produce and was a triumph. It was grand and colorful and muscular. Turner's effort, by comparison, looked gray and weedy. The working-class painter from London sized the two pictures up and decided some action was required if his reputation as the country's greatest living artist was not to be lost to his more refined and socially acceptable adversary, John Constable. Turner reached for his paints, selected the brightest red he could find, plunged his brush into the sticky mass, and then brandished it in front of his canvas like a sword.

He made one purposeful stab into the heart of *Helvoetsluys* and retreated. He watched as the thick blob of blood-like paint started to seep into the canvas, transforming it from what had been a slightly dull image into a far more vibrant affair, a picture that could now stand comparison with Constable's great work. The daub—which Turner said represented a buoy—was no bigger than a cufflink, but had the desired effect. When Constable saw what his rival had done, he exclaimed, "He has been here and fired a gun!"

Turner's improvised response is not unusual for an artist, but nor is it universal. There are some, like Marcel Duchamp, who prefer to take to their chair and remain there for a very long time while pondering a work in progress. The Frenchman was a famously thoughtful artist who was as much a philosopher as he was a painter or sculptor. He was not one to rush or be prone to impulsiveness: a character trait to which his final work bears testament.

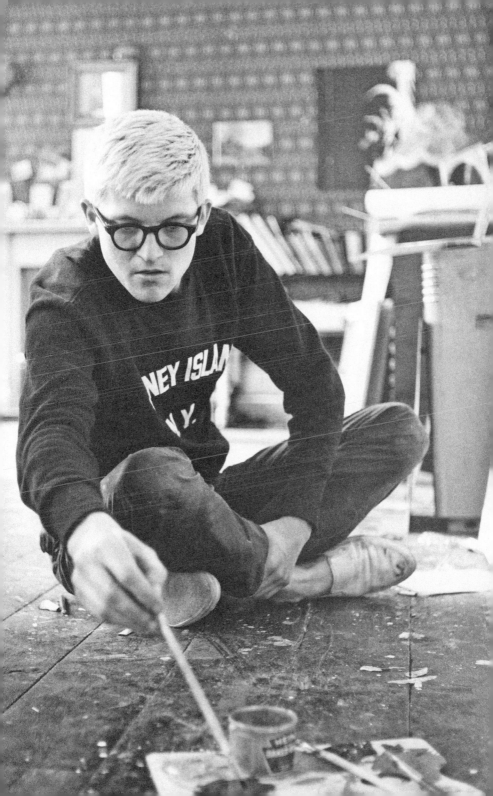

"ART IS NOT ABOUT ITSELF BUT THE ATTENTION WE BRING TO IT."

Marcel Duchamp

Étant Donnés (1946–66) is a masterpiece of erotic symbolism that has become an icon for artists the world over. It was an homage to this late work by Duchamp that I saw hanging loosely from the wall in Luc Tuymans's studio when I visited. The Belgian artist had painted his version in a single day. Duchamp took twenty years to make the original.

In those two decades he spent sitting in his chair, thinking about *Étant Donnés* and playing endless games of chess, he would occasionally make an amendment or an addition to his elaborate artwork. It is a typically cryptic piece made from an assortment of objects and materials including nails, bricks, velvet, wood, twigs and rubber. You couldn't really call it a sculpture, it's more of a stage set, or what is now commonly known as an installation artwork—an entirely new concept at the time.

You view the piece by peering through a small hole in an old, wooden Spanish door. What you see is weirdly surreal, reminiscent of a murder scene in a David Lynch movie. In the foreground is a brick wall that has been bashed through to reveal a naked woman lying spread-eagled on her back. Her head, right arm and feet are not visible. But her torso, legs and left arm are all clearly in view. She is as pale as marble, and one would assume dead if it were not for the gas lamp she is holding up in her left hand. The broken twigs and crinkled old leaves upon which her body rests are made to look all the more creepy by the bucolic beauty of the rolling hills and assorted pine trees in the distance (a backdrop Duchamp created by retouching an old photograph).

If ever there was an artwork that was made by an artist pausing for thought, it is *Étant Donnés*. And if ever there was an artist to inspire those of us who doubt our own creativity it was Marcel Duchamp.

Technically speaking, he was very limited. His brother was a much better sculptor and most of the other painters in Paris at the time—including Picasso and Matisse—were far, far more accomplished. To that extent, Duchamp was not a great artist. His genius was that he learned how to think like one.

A brief look back at the chapters of this book shows how he did it. Was he enterprising? I should say so. This was the man who moved to New York and used his Gallic charm to woo rich American ladies to support him and his endeavors, and would go on to produce a bottle of perfume that contained nothing but thin air. And when he encountered the prospect of failure because of his limited technical talents, he simply moved on to Plan B and reinvented himself as the world's first conceptual artist.

Duchamp's trick was to spend more time thinking than doing.

As for being seriously curious, well, few could match Duchamp's inquiring mind. He read prodigiously, was an influential force in every art movement from Dada to Pop, played chess to a national standard, and made sure he was a constant presence among the intellectuals of Europe and America. And he wasn't above stealing either. The exposed position of the naked woman in *Étant Donnés* was not his original idea; it was taken from Gustave Courbet's painting *The Origin of the World* (1866).

That he was brave, there is no doubt. He challenged the core beliefs of the all-powerful art world, risking both his reputation and his livelihood. His courage paid off. He fundamentally changed not only the course of art history, but also that of culture more broadly. Surrealism, Monty Python, and even punk rock owe something to him. How did he do it? By being skeptical. Why should art be beautiful, he asked. And why does it have to be made by an artist? His answer to these questions was to buy a urinal and declare it a "ready-made" sculpture, and in so doing he paved the way for Andy Warhol, Jeff Koons, Damien Hirst and Ai Weiwei, among many others.

You can see from *Étant Donnés* how Duchamp thought both big picture and fine detail. Here is a large, sprawling artwork that you can only see through a tiny hole. And that hole represented his point of view. He couldn't understand why artists allowed people to look at their work from whatever angle the viewer chose. Duchamp thought he should determine precisely how someone saw his work, and made sure that was the case in his final masterpiece, which can only be seen from one very specific, static viewpoint.

Duchamp is a worthy role model. Added to which he believed passionately that anyone could be an artist and spent his life showing the rest of us how it is done. He chose fine art as the vehicle for his imagination, but his approach could equally well be applied to any area of creative endeavor.

His trick was to spend more time thinking than doing. He would pause for thought and ponder on life and creativity and how things might be. Which is what I'm going to do now.

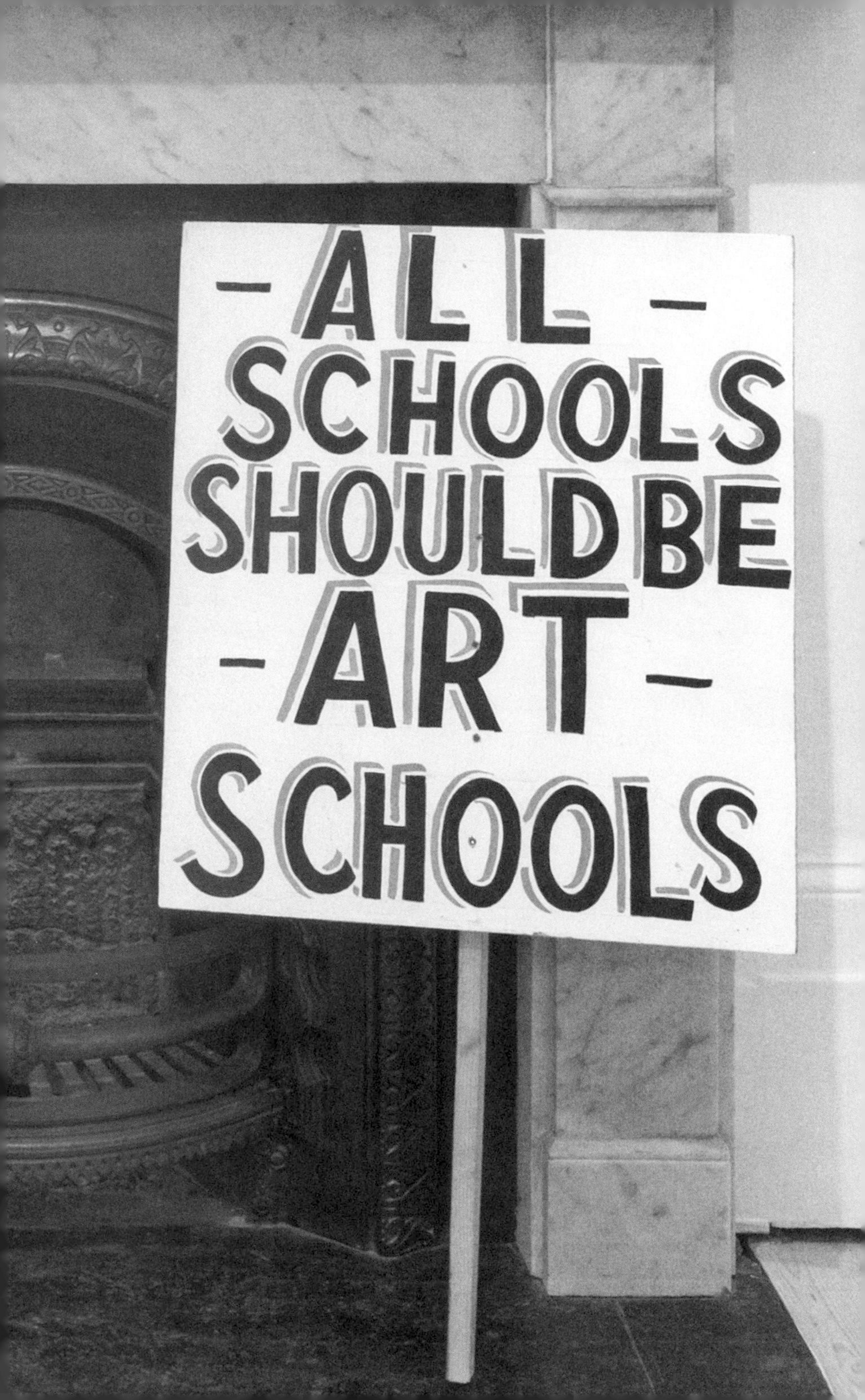
ALL
SCHOOLS
SHOULD BE
ART
SCHOOLS

10. ALL SCHOOLS SHOULD BE ART SCHOOLS

All Schools Should Be Art Schools (2013) is a painting by a British artist who trades under the pseudonym Bob and Roberta Smith. He made it for the launch of his Art Party, a single-issue lobby that consists of a loose grouping of artists who are concerned about the diminishing role of the arts and design in English schools. To that extent his campaign is quite specific, but his provocation is interesting beyond that. Perhaps all schools should be art schools—at least in attitude rather than curriculum?

Whatever the outcome of Bob and Roberta Smith's efforts, it does seem like a good time to be asking the question. After all, if our future is indeed going to be based on a creative economy, and more of our spare time dedicated to making, then it would appear sensible to prepare young people accordingly.

I'm not suggesting there isn't already much to admire in our current systems of formal education, just that there is always room for some innovation. Particularly when you take into account the disruptive effects of the digital revolution, which is creating numerous opportunities to reimagine how education might be delivered and received in the future.

Schools and universities around the world have been quick to recognize the challenges and possibilities brought about by the digital age. We have seen the advent of MOOCs (Massive Open Online Courses), which provide freely accessible web lectures given by internationally respected subject specialists. And then there's the notion of the "flipped classroom," where pupils use the physical space of school or university as a social platform to share and develop ideas, while utilizing the Internet as a place to receive old-school one-to-one lectures.

These initiatives are liberating in their own way, and are likely to help students become independently minded and self-reliant, two big steps towards developing a culture of creativity. But I think Bob and Roberta Smith's vision goes slightly further. It is based on his own experience at art school, which, he says, taught him "how to think, not what to think."

He studied art at Goldsmiths College in London in the early 1990s, when it was possibly the most famous art school in the world. A couple of years earlier it had spawned

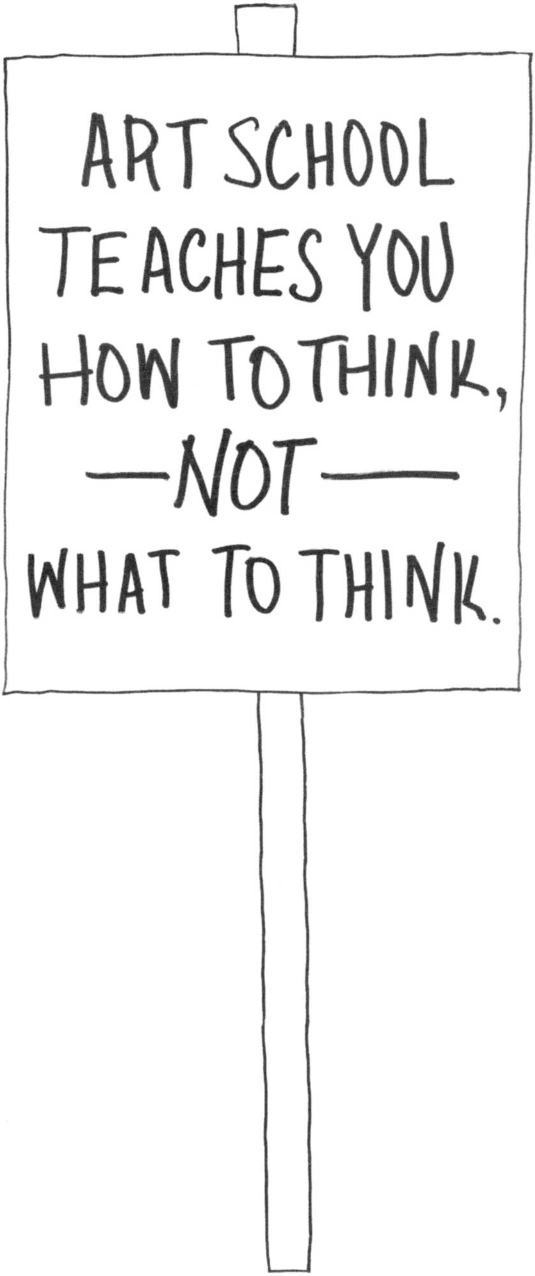
ART SCHOOL
TEACHES YOU
HOW TO THINK,
—NOT—
WHAT TO THINK.

a group of publicity-seeking, establishment-baiting artists who would go on to be known as YBA (Young British Artists). Their leader was a dynamic, cocky young student called Damien Hirst, who, as we know, has become one of the most successful artists of his generation.

Goldsmiths was the making of Hirst; he was a star student. And yet he arrived there with a terrible secondary school art grade, the lowest you can achieve and still scrape a pass. Why did one of the world's most influential, innovative and enterprising artists not do well at school? Why did someone like Damien Hirst blossom at art college and not before?

Bob and Roberta Smith thinks the root cause of the problem is the narrow body of knowledge taught in schools, which over generations has been codified into a set of rules enclosed within finite boundaries. But art—and by extension creativity—he says, "is all about breaking rules" and "discovering new stuff."

Why did someone like Damien Hirst blossom at art college and not before?

There is, of course, a paradox in the notion that students should go to school to learn how to break rules, but maybe it is worth contemplating. It might help overcome an even greater paradox embedded in the current education system, which Bob and Roberta Smith points out can unintentionally place a limit on the intellectual development of students.

In many classrooms around the world, students will sit in lessons and be told about the scientific discoveries of Einstein and Galileo, the plays of Shakespeare and the exploits of Napoleon. They will listen and learn and take notes. And then they will be given a test in which they are asked to recount what they have been told. Yet the reason they are learning about these individuals in the first place is because Einstein, Galileo, Shakespeare and Napoleon all achieved great things by ignoring conventional wisdom and being brave enough to question long-held assumptions. In other words, they excelled because they didn't do as they were told. Could it be that students learn what these great minds achieved, but not always the far more valuable lesson of how they did it?

Could it be that students learn what these great minds achieved, but not always the far more valuable lesson of how they did it?

Art school helped Bob and Roberta Smith to think independently and to develop the confidence to generate his own ideas in response to studying a problem. He was taught to look, understand, judge, and then produce a physical object that addressed the issues he wanted to explore. The "facts" were the starting point, not the conclusion. It was what he did with the information he had been given that mattered. The method, materials and medium were all up to him— as was his interpretation. The assumption being that life is uncertain and there is never a single answer. All things need to be considered, and different points of view are inevitable.

It makes you wonder about the real value of our current system of public exams, which are based on regurgitating received information. Obviously the basics have to be learned, and some form of test or examination is useful. But should such tests be based mainly on knowledge retention, as they generally are today? Isn't that a bit of a blunt tool when almost every fact you're ever going to need to know is but a mouse click away? Added to which, isn't there the risk that these exams only expose what a young person doesn't know, as opposed to providing an opportunity for them to show off what they do know? Might that fear of public humiliation— for both student and academic institution—stop creativity in its tracks? Could it be that exams don't open students' eyes but instead attach a pair of blinkers?

Maybe rewarding new and interesting rather than right or wrong would help develop more of the skills needed for a creative economy.

What if the status of creativity in schools and universities were elevated? Academic institutions might then feel encouraged to take an art school type approach to education by focusing the curriculum more on projects that the students have helped define and less on exams. Maybe rewarding new and interesting rather than right or wrong would help develop more of the skills needed for a creative economy. Such an approach would give students more opportunity to critique each other's work, in discussions facilitated by a teacher whose role wasn't necessarily to have all the answers, but to ensure a Socratic-like interaction that would lead to revelations and progress. The aim would not be to ridicule or belittle, but to expand horizons, identify problems and iron out inconsistencies.

This was Bob and Roberta Smith's experience at art school, where he learned how to be critical and how to be criticized, a process that taught him intellectual rigor and emotional resilience, both of which are absolutely essential in any sphere of creativity. He left, he said, as all students should leave education: self-aware and self-assured.

I suspect that there is an informality to art schools that is conducive to creativity. Clearly, that's not always easy in the realm of primary and secondary education, but could it be an aim nevertheless? Might it be possible for schools to be considered more like centers for creativity and self-discovery as opposed to a mild form of state-enforced incarceration?

An art school mentality might not only teach students how to have good ideas, but also engender the enterprising attitude required to realize them. It is assumed at many art colleges that most students are likely to end up achieving their ambitions through self-employment. So, instead of corporate milk rounds, practice job interviews, and worrying about how to second-guess a future boss, art students are taught how to make and do.

"Creativity is contagious, pass it on." Albert Einstein

This already happens within the existing structures in art schools, but a more student-focused approach might now be feasible in our digital age. Could we not start to build a semi-bespoke curriculum tailored to the tastes and interests of individual students? It hasn't been possible in the past for practical reasons of resources and exam requirements. But with the rapidly advancing technological aids, combined with a less exam-centric approach, the opportunity for a change in emphasis might present itself.

How viable is the one-size-fits-all model for a future for a generation of students who have grown up using technology to curate their lives and interests? By the time many of them arrive at high school they have already personalized their world with playlists, Facebook homepages, and Google filters. To persist with a linear system of top-down education might feel increasingly like putting a finger in the digital dam: a dam about to burst with the millions of individuals demanding bespoke learning.

Art schools, which admittedly are generally catering for a sixteen-plus student, are apt to be a little more accommodating. Teachers are able to act as enablers and collaborators, and not so much as law enforcers and examiners. And with that comes the freedom to try and help students find an area of personal interest through which the whole world starts to make sense. That's not possible when everything is geared towards public exams, but might work if the test-orientated system were loosened up a bit.

> "Every child is an artist, the problem is staying an artist when you grow up." Pablo Picasso

Art school or not, students need to leave education as independently minded, intellectually curious, self-confident and resourceful individuals who feel prepared for, and excited by, the future and what they might be able to contribute to it. That is not always the case today. Young people can leave school with a diminished sense of themselves, feeling like failures and short on confidence. I'm not sure that works for anyone.

Would it be any better if all schools were art schools? I think so. But whatever your view, there are few more exciting areas than education in our digital age. I know tech and media and neuroscience are sexier, but for sheer untapped potential that is waiting to be realized by a new generation of thinkers and doers, I doubt there's anything to beat education as a place to work right now.

So much is about to change, including, I would have thought, our relationship with academia. A combination of an intellectually ambitious aging population, an emerging creative economy, and a digitized world will lead to many of us renewing or expanding our ties with education. The notion that formal learning stops when we are barely adults will seem very odd in future. As will the idea that someone has one single career for life. If you're going to be working until you're eighty, the chances are you'll want to explore several fields and not plow the same furrow decade after decade.

And that will mean going back to school or college or university. And there we will find that these academic institutions, with their incredible talent and resources to share with the world, are no longer walled gardens with "Keep Out" signs, but open and exciting hubs offering us an intellectually charged socket into which we can all plug when in need of inspiration, knowledge and a chance to think.

"YOU CAN'T WAIT FOR INSPIRATION, YOU HAVE TO GO AFTER IT WITH A CLUB."

Jack London

11. A FINAL THOUGHT

If all schools should be art schools, maybe all offices should be artists' studios. I'm not suggesting people should start coming to work wearing blue smocks with pockets stuffed full of paintbrushes, but I do think if fostering creativity is a genuine goal for businesses then the work environment should feel more collaborative and less hierarchical.

A creative economy needs independently minded individuals with the freedom and capacity to think imaginatively.

All those innovative, aspiring twenty-first-century enterprises say they need people who can conceive ideas of value and know how to realize them. And yet the majority of businesses still retain traditional authoritarian structures. There are exceptions, of course. The American animation company Pixar springs to mind, with its Brains Trust, feedback forums, and open invitation to employees to come up with ideas for a screenplay.

But such instances are still quite rare. Companies are not set up in an optimal way to create the conditions where staff have the opportunity and confidence to express their talents if the employer–employee relationship is largely based on subordination, not collaboration. Being employed can be a stifling and infantilizing experience, which is hardly conducive to creativity.

But what if we had an economy more akin to the one in which artists operate, where the majority of people are self-employed? Each of us would have our own speciality, operating with the enterprising mindset of an artist. Businesses would still exist, big and small, but we would no longer work for them, we would work with them. The association might last for twenty years or twenty minutes. True, the full-time employee's sense of security would be lost (often a delusion anyway), but it would be exchanged for a greater sense of self and independence.

This scenario is already a reality for millions of freelancers across the world, but they continue to be the exception, not the norm. And in most cases they are still viewed as outsiders, fringe players, and specialist hired help, as opposed to being an integral part of a business. I doubt that would still be the case if the majority of people were free agents: the dynamics of employment, and, by extension, society, would change.

The upside would be a highly motivated, extremely creative, flexible workforce who felt masters of their own destiny: a new generation empowered by their careers. The challenge would be the need to design new support structures to help a population of freelancers enjoy the good times and survive the bad ones.

I suspect it would prompt a review into the nature of the current systems of remuneration. The added value and exceptional skills provided by this community of creatives would need to be taken into account. Incentives or bonuses are fine as far as they go, but shouldn't there be a more equitable share of the spoils? If the freelancers are sharing the risk by not being full-time employees, then perhaps they ought to share the upside too?

If you have helped create or develop a commercial service or product, should you have a share in it that is commensurate with your contribution? Perhaps the current convention that sees freelancers sign over their intellectual property rights should be changed too? Could it be replaced with a new system that represents a more proportionate way of sharing wealth, which recognizes and rewards the creative majority and not just the executive minority?

Even from the position of a casual observer, it seems increasingly obvious that there is a developing trend towards the mega and the micro. The middling, the so-so and the average are finding life harder in the world of instant online feedback and vast consumer choice offered by our global economy. Okay is no longer OK.

There is a clear division opening up. On one side there are the global super-brands, huge out-of-town shopping districts, and dominant websites; while on the other there are the artisans making and providing authentic, bespoke and local products and services. Many of these skilled craftsmen and women are trading from their local main street in shops that were once boarded up. It is this growing band of individuals and small collectives that is evolving into the new creative class.

**"A room hung with pictures is a room hung with thoughts."
Sir Joshua Reynolds**

Perhaps we are already edging towards a society that will once again be filled with cabinet-makers and artisan bakers, Sunday painters and part-time inventors—most of whom will be working in or benefiting from the digital world. The false divide between the creative haves and have-nots will finally be removed as we come to realize that everyone has the gift for producing imaginative work of merit.

I think it is reasonable to argue that the shift towards a broader creative community is already happening in business. It is said, for example, that last year more start-up businesses were founded by enterprising entrepreneurs than ever before. Some will become rich and famous, like Facebook's Mark Zuckerberg; others will remain less well known. It is quite possible that the twenty-year-old woman who served you a coffee this morning is a part-time app designer of note, and that the young guy who emptied your trash last Friday is the lead singer of a band with an impressive international online following.

More and more people I meet, young and old, have taken up a creative sideline or two. Some are happy enough to combine their making lives with their working lives, while others support themselves with a portfolio of jobs and enterprises. And then there are those who have been able to establish their creative concern so successfully that it financially supports them.

This is the sort of professional balancing act that artists have perfected over the centuries. They are well used to combining their art practice with a more secure job such as teaching. It is a high risk/low risk mix that I can see becoming a more common model across society. It could be that the time-honored system of a single boss overseeing a strict hierarchy in which full-time employees obediently fit into the corporate straitjacket will start to seem very old-fashioned. Particularly for any business that prizes or profits from creativity. A traditional system based on a vertical chain of command is the optimum way to run an army, or a chain-gang, precisely because it is a sure-fire way of suppressing the human imagination.

The future depends on us taking a different approach. One in which we can all express ourselves and contribute to society by using our unique imagination and talent. It's our brains not our brawn that makes us special and life worth living. Artists had that worked out a long time ago.

"THE MAIN THING IS TO BE MOVED, TO LOVE, TO HOPE, TO TREMBLE, TO LIVE."

Auguste Rodin

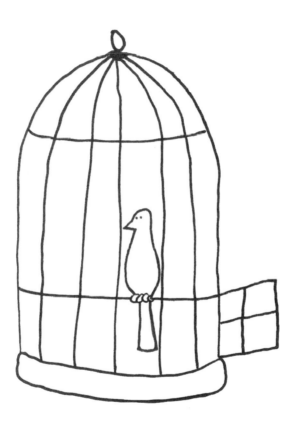

Acknowledgments

First and foremost I'd like to thank you for buying this book. I hope you found at least some passages within it chimed with you, either in observations made or anecdotes told.

It's been a while in gestation. Maybe all my adult life. A long time, certainly. Which means that a lot of people have been involved in shaping it—and me—along the way.

Paul Richardson is one. He was the kind-hearted man who took me on as a stage-hand at Sadler's Wells in the mid-1980s, when I had nothing to offer other than enthusiasm. He showed me how to "run" a thirty-foot-high, flat-fronted piece of scenery from one side of the stage to the other without coming a cropper. He was also the first person to introduce me to artists.

Gee Thompson is another. He shared my interest in creativity and together we published a magazine called *SHOTS* in the early 1990s. It was about the craft of making short films such as commercials and pop videos. We sold it—probably unwisely and certainly too soon—but I am delighted it continues to this day.

And then there is Steve Hare, to whom this book is dedicated. He taught me—and everybody lucky enough to know him—about the thrilling beauty of having an inquiring mind. He was an extraordinarily intelligent, kind and generous person, a man totally devoid of avarice, pettiness or insincerity. He was also the world's foremost expert on Penguin, the original publisher of this book.

Penguin is now a very big company, following its merger with Random House. Not everybody was happy with the union, but I was delighted. It means that my dear friend Bill

Scott-Kerr, a brilliant publisher at Random House, is now not only a drinking buddy and sounding board, but also a bona-fide colleague.

As is Ben Brusey, my first editor at Viking. His mentor was the softly spoken, ultra-smart Joel Rickett, a publisher at the imprint. When Ben moved onwards and upwards within the Group, Joel kindly agreed to take up the reins with me. I'm flattered and honored.

Big publishers are often criticized for being impersonal and uncaring. That is not my experience at Penguin. Joanna Prior and Venetia Butterfield are a dream team to work with. They are thoughtful, supportive, incredibly dedicated and great fun. As is Annie Lee, the book's copy-editor, with whom I can happily pass hours chatting about art and artists. I'm also incredibly fortunate to have benefited from Richard Bravery's graphic design talent, Huw Armstrong's picture research and Emma Brown's patience.

You can't write a book about artists without artists. I'm immensely grateful to all those painters, performers, thinkers and sculptors who have been willing to spend time with me over the years, and to the organizations which made such meetings possible, most recently the Tate Gallery and the BBC.

Ultimately, creativity is about optimism and love. And there is nobody who embodies the two more profoundly than Kate, my wife. She has a razor-sharp mind that can immediately spot a phony line or dodgy syntax, an ability she appears to have passed on to our children, who have pitched in from time to time with face-saving suggestions. If there are any good bits it's down to them—the howlers are all mine.

Illustration and Photographic Credits

BLACK AND WHITE

p. 12: photograph © Jack Berman/Moment/Getty Images; **p. 20:** photograph © Susie Cushner/Taxi/Getty Images; **p. 23:** photograph © Mondadori/Getty Images; **p. 25:** Andy Warhol, *Dollar Sign*, *c.* 1981 © The Andy Warhol Foundation for the Visual Arts, Inc./DACS; **pp. 34–5:** Theaster Gates, *Dorchester Projects*, 2009 © White Cube, London, 2015; **p. 38:** photograph © B. SCHMID/Amana Images/Getty Images; **p. 44:** photograph © Evening Standard/Hulton Archive/Getty Images; **p. 50:** Roy Lichtenstein, *Washington Crossing the Delaware I*, *c.* 1951 © The Estate of Roy Lichtenstein/DACS, 2015. Image courtesy of the Gagosian Gallery. Photograph: Robert McKeever; **p. 54:** photograph © Ogilvy & Mather, all rights reserved; **p. 58:** photograph © Jeffrey Coolidge/Stone/Getty Images; **p. 65:** Marina Abramović, Ulay, *Breathing In/Breathing Out*, 1977 © Marina Abramović, 2015. Courtesy of Marina Abramović and Sean Kelly Gallery, New York and DACS; **p. 68:** photograph © Gilbert & George. All rights reserved, DACS, 2015. Photograph: Gilbert & George Studio; **p. 71:** Peter Fischli/David Weiss, *How to Work Better*, 1991 © Peter Fischli and David Weiss, courtesy of Matthew Marks Gallery, New York; **p. 78:** photograph © Godong/Robert Harding World Imagery/Getty Images; **p. 82:** photograph © Keystone-France/Gamma-Keystone/Getty Images; **p. 89:** photograph © Gjon Mili/Masters/Getty Images; **p. 94:** Pablo Picasso, from *The Bull* (*La Taureau*), 1945–6 © Succession Picasso/DACS, London, 2015/Museum of Fine Arts, Boston/Museum of Modern Art, New York/Art Resource/Scala, Florence; **p. 120:** photograph author's own; **pp. 126–7:** photographs author's own; **p. 139:** photograph © Tim Robberts/Stone/Getty Images; **p. 144:** Otto Dix, from *Der Krieg*, 1924 © 2015 DACS/The Metropolitan Museum of Art/Art Resource/Scala, Florence; **p. 145:** Francisco Goya, from *The Disasters of War*, 1810–20 © Image, The Metropolitan Museum of Art/Art Resource/Scala, Florence; **p. 152:** Rembrandt van Rijn, *The Night Watch*, 1642 © Rijksmuseum, Amsterdam, 2015; **p. 158:** photograph © Andy Crawford/Dorling Kindserley/Getty Images; **p. 161:** photograph © KAMMERMAN/Gamma-Rapho/Getty Images; **p. 171:** Banksy, *Wall Art*, 2005 © British Museum; **p. 176:** photograph © Henrik Sorensen/The Image Bank/Getty Images; **p. 179:** photograph © Tony Evans/Timelapse Library Ltd/Hulton Archive/Getty Images; **p. 180:** photograph © Eliot Elisofon/The LIFE Picture Collection/Getty Images; **p. 184:** Bob and Roberta Smith, from *All Schools Should Be Art Schools*, 2013 © Bob and Roberta Smith, 2015; **p. 194:** photograph © LWA/Larry Williams/Blend Images/Getty Images.

COLOR

Bridget Riley, *Man with a Red Turban (After van Eyck)*, 1946 © Bridget Riley, 2015. All rights reserved, courtesy of Karsten Shubert, London; Bridget Riley, *Pink Landscape*, 1960 © Bridget Riley, 2015. All rights reserved, courtesy of Karsten Shubert, London; Bridget Riley, *Kiss*, 1961 © Bridget Riley, 2015. All rights reserved, courtesy of Karsten Shubert, London; Michelangelo Merisi da Caravaggio, *Self Portrait as the Sick Bacchus*, 1593 © Image, Galleria Borghese, Rome/Scala, Florence; Caravaggio, *The Supper at Emmaus*, 1601 © The National Gallery, London. Presented by the Hon. George Vernon, 1839; Caravaggio, *Salome with the Head of John the Baptist*, 1607 © The National Gallery, London; Pablo Picasso, *Dwarf Dancer*, 1901 © Succession Picasso/DACS, London, 2015/Museo Picasso, Barcelona, Spain/The Bridgeman Art Library; Pablo Picasso, *Seated Harlequin*, 1901 © Succession Picasso/DACS, London, 2015/The Metropolitan Museum of Art/Art Resource/Scala, Florence; Jacques-Louis David, *The Death of Socrates*, 1787 © Image, The Metropolitan Museum of Art, 2015/Art Resource/Scala, Florence; Piero della Francesca, *Flagellation of Christ*, 1458–60 © Galleria Nazionale delle Marche, Urbino, Italy/The Bridgeman Art Library; Luc Tuymans, *William Robertson*, 2014 © courtesy David Zwirner, New York/London and Zeno X Gallery, Antwerp; Luc Tuymans, *John Robison*, 2014 © courtesy David Zwirner, New York/London and Zeno X Gallery, Antwerp; Luc Tuymans, *John Playfair*, 2014 © courtesy David Zwirner, New York/London and Zeno X Gallery, Antwerp; Johannes Vermeer, *Girl with a Pearl Earring*, 1665 © Mauritshuis, The Hague; Peter Doig, *Ski Jacket*, 1994 © Peter Doig. All rights reserved, DACS, 2015/TATE Modern, London; Rembrandt van Rijn, *Self Portrait at the Age of 63*, 1669 © The National Gallery, London; Kerry James Marshall, *De Style*, 1993 © Digital Image Museum Associates/Los Angeles County Museum of Art/Art Resource/Scala, Florence & Jack Shainman Gallery, New York, 2015.

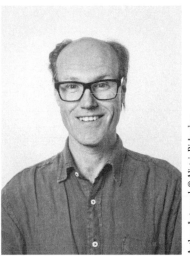

Author photograph © Alistair Richardson

As the BBC's Arts Editor, Will Gompertz has interviewed and observed many of the world's leading artists, directors, novelists, musicians, actors and designers. *Creativity Magazine* in New York ranked him as one of the fifty most original thinkers in the world.

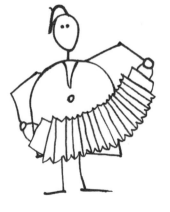